George Washington's Leadership Lessons

George Washington's Leadership Lessons

What the Father of Our Country
Can Teach Us About Effective
Leadership and Character

James C. Rees

Executive Director of Mount Vernon
with Stephen Spignesi

John Wiley & Sons, Inc.

Published by John Wiley & Sons, Inc., Hoboken, New Jersey
Published simultaneously in Canada

For general information on our other products and services or for technical support, please contact our Customer Care Department within the United States at (800) 762-2974, outside the United States at (317) 572-3993 or fax (317) 572-4002.

Wiley also publishes its books in a variety of electronic formats. Some content that appears in print may not be available in electronic books. For more information about Wiley products, visit our web site at www.wiley.com

Library of Congress Cataloging-in-Publication Data:

Rees, James C.
  George Washington's leadership lessons : what the father of our country can teach us about effective leadership and character / James C. Rees with Stephen Spignesi.
    p. cm.
  Includes bibliographical references.
  ISBN-13: 978-0-470-08887-6 (cloth)
  1. Leadership. 2. Washington, George, 1732–1799. I. Spignesi, Stephen J. II. Title.
  HD57.7.R436 2007
  658.4'092—dc22   2006030751

Printed in the United States of America

10 9 8 7 6 5 4 3 2 1

*To the eighteen dedicated leaders who have served
as Regents of the Mount Vernon Ladies' Association,
1853–2006*

Contents

Preface: Footsteps to Follow   xi

Acknowledgments   xvii

Introduction: The Mark of a Leader   xxi

PART I
Leadership Lessons   1

Leadership Lesson 1	A Leader Has Vision	3
Leadership Lesson 2	A Leader Is Honest	11
Leadership Lesson 3	A Leader Has Ambition	19
Leadership Lesson 4	A Leader Is Courageous	27
Leadership Lesson 5	A Leader Has Self-Control	33
Leadership Lesson 6	A Leader Takes Personal Responsibility	39
Leadership Lesson 7	A Leader Is Determined	47
Leadership Lesson 8	A Leader Has a Strong Work Ethic	53
Leadership Lesson 9	A Leader Uses Good Judgment	59
Leadership Lesson 10	A Leader Learns from Mistakes	69
Leadership Lesson 11	A Leader Is Humble	77
Leadership Lesson 12	A Leader Does the Research and Development	85
Leadership Lesson 13	A Leader Values Presentation	91
Leadership Lesson 14	A Leader Exceeds Expectations	99
Leadership Lesson 15	A Leader Has Heartfelt Faith	103

PART II
The Rules of Civility   111

PART III
George Washington, Entrepreneur   145

Notes   183
Selected Bibliography   195
Resources   199
About the Authors   201
Index   203

America has furnished to the world the character of Washington, and if our American institutions had done nothing else, that alone would have entitled them to the respect of mankind.

—DANIEL WEBSTER

He was greater than any of us believed he was.

—DOUGLAS SOUTHALL FREEMAN

Preface
Footsteps to Follow

Attention must be paid . . .
—ARTHUR MILLER, *Death of a Salesman*

C hange is inevitable, but some things should never be left behind, never be forgotten. With his face still so familiar, so seen by our eyes and touched by our fingers every day, it seems highly unlikely that George Washington is in any danger of becoming just a footnote in history.

But over the past four decades, Americans have clearly begun to take "The Father of Our Country" for granted. In fact, his face may be the only aspect of Washington that remains famous. Washington's status in the mind-set of Americans has slowly but surely drifted from that of a genuine hero and effective role model to that of a patriotic symbol, like the Stars and Stripes or the American eagle.

Not long ago I explained this predicament to a very successful corporate executive whose home and office were both within 20 minutes of George Washington's estate. In his mid-30s, this brilliant and aggressive entrepreneur had bought and sold two firms and pocketed some $200 million. Rumors were flying that he was about to announce the start-up of still another new venture. Unfortunately, he had never visited Mount Vernon. And his response to my explanation about Washington's fade from prominence was simple: "So what?"

A reasonable question perhaps. After all, the world has changed so much since Washington died in 1799. Is it possible that Washington's life and accomplishments are no longer relevant?

Certainly it is true that an examination of Washington's taste in clothes or his favorite foods may no longer be a worthwhile use of anyone's time. But in the grander sense, Washington's greatest contributions to America—his leadership and character—are as relevant and valuable today as they have ever been. In fact, there are those who argue that America is experiencing such a drought in terms of leadership that Washington's example may be more critical now than it was two centuries ago.

Most scholars seem to understand this. In a recent poll of historians conducted by the *Wall Street Journal,* George Washington was once again selected as our greatest president. But when "man in the street" surveys are conducted, "The Father of Our Country" typically drops to seventh or eighth place. In one of the most recent public opinion polls, Americans ranked both Bill Clinton and George W. Bush ahead of our first president—you have to ask yourself, what were they thinking?

Hard to believe, yes. But undeniably true. There is a tremendous disconnect between George Washington and the American people, and this gap involves both the mind and the heart. Younger people, in particular, know very little about Washington's achievements, and what they do know is often more myth than reality. Another recent survey showed that 65 percent of college seniors don't know who commanded the American forces at Yorktown.

And Americans no longer embrace Washington with the same genuine sense of patriotism that they did even 50 years ago.

At Mount Vernon, we wanted to understand why this is happening—why are Americans losing touch with the true essence of George Washington? The answer to this question is more quantifiable than you might imagine.

➤ Washington has been pushed to the back burner in school systems across the country. His portrait has disappeared from classroom walls, and history textbooks now have as little as 10 percent of the coverage of Washington that they possessed just 40 years ago. That's why author David McCullough has bemoaned that we are "raising a generation of historically illiterate children."

➤ George Washington's Birthday, once one of the most important and successful holidays of the year, has all but vanished. Seniors frequently tell me about the George Washington's Birthday parades they viewed as children and the school assemblies that featured skits about Washington's honesty and goodness. Washington was a unifying figure for American families, not just the nation as a whole. But Presidents' Day has allowed the grain to fall aside, leaving us with nothing but the chaff. If our government leaders who traded George Washington's Birthday for Presidents' Day thought for a second that meaningful discussions about presidential leadership would take place, they were wildly off target. Instead, we have been forced to watch ridiculous costumed versions of George Washington and Abraham Lincoln hawking new cars and appliance sales during a three-day shopping extravaganza.

➤ In terms of relative interest, in America, history is dwindling among the general public. In the 1960s, as many as 1.3 million people annually visited Mount Vernon. By 2005, that number had shrunk to 950,000. But still, Mount Vernon is doing significantly better than many other history-related sites. Colonial Williamsburg and Monticello have faced far more serious declines, and some living history sites are nearing a crisis situation. Americans are traveling more often, and to faraway places, but it is absolutely clear that traditional historic sites have not been the beneficiaries of this trend.

In my opinion, we have created a vicious cycle that is truly dangerous to our nation's future. It starts in the classroom, where far less time and attention is given to American history. In turn, parents feel less inclined to commit vacation time to historic places. And given a vote—which they usually are in today's world—children seldom opt for history over theme parks, water worlds, and shopping malls.

As a result, younger generations of Americans don't know much about their own history. And with knowledge comes respect. So, sadly, the greatest leaders our nation has ever known have been marginalized, virtually removed from a meaningful place in our society.

Even those who should be the most knowledgeable about George Washington seem to be following the public's lead. Although The White House is just 16 miles from George Washington's home, President Bill Clinton never entered our gates—though invited dozens of times—during eight years in office. As of late 2006, President George W. Bush has yet to find the time to improve upon this record. This is another break from past tradition—our archives are overflowing with photographs of former presidents escorting world leaders, as well as family and friends, to what they often referred to as "a national shrine."

Over the past several years, we have been thrilled that several of America's most accomplished historians—David Hackett Fischer, Joseph Ellis, and David McCullough—have written glowing accounts of Washington's achievements. These books have sold well—more than a million copies in some cases. But I am convinced that the same 3 or 4 million history buffs—those same people who have made The History Channel such a success—are reading all of these books, usually with great enthusiasm.

But that means that about 295 million Americans are not being exposed to American history—and leaders like George Washington—in an effective fashion. From the highest levels of leaders to the newest immigrant reciting his first Pledge of Allegiance, it is clear to me that we are not encouraging Americans to learn from their past like we should be.

This book was not written for that choir of 3 to 4 million devoted fans of American history. There already exist a remarkable number of good books on George Washington, written by scholars who are far more insightful than yours truly. Stephen Spignesi and I have tried to create a book that is concise and compelling enough to interest those who have never had an opportunity to see Washington as a relevant role model. Simply put, we believe that George Washington can be used as an example of strong and ethical leadership in virtually any walk of life. His footsteps are still there to be followed, and we hope to convince a few people to begin this journey, which we feel is a rewarding and important one.

Acknowledgments

JAMES C. REES

*T*here are a number of people whose talents and expertise influenced and informed this book. Dr. Dennis
Pogue and Mount Vernon's trusted miller, Joel Nichols,
helped to fine-tune the text on George Washington's entrepreneurial ventures. Anne Johnson juggled and reconfig-
ured the manuscript on a daily basis, with great aplomb,
and Dawn Bonner was the creative force behind the selec-
tion of illustrations.

Most of all, Mary Thompson, whose knowledge of
George Washington and his Mount Vernon home is as
encyclopedic as anyone I have ever known, suggested
numerous enhancements to the manuscript. She gave
freely of her ideas about Washington's true personality,
as she has so many times before in her 25 remarkable
years on the Mount Vernon staff.

I have had the privilege of hearing lectures, participating in roundtable sessions, and occasionally breaking
bread with a long list of Washington scholars. Some have
thought more of Washington's leadership than others, of
course, but the cumulative effect is clear–Washington's
stock has risen precipitously over the past decade, much

to my surprise and delight. David McCullough, in particular, has established a connection between historical figures and the American people that is vibrant and meaningful.

Unlike most historic sites, Mount Vernon is totally independent—we do not receive government support of any kind. As a result, private support is essential to Mount Vernon's survival. Fortunately, a number of corporate leaders have adopted Mount Vernon as one of their priority causes, and in the process, I have had the pleasure of meeting a number of incredible leaders in action. Fred W. Smith, who headed Donrey Media Group before chairing the Donald W. Reynolds Foundation, is one of the most decisive leaders I have ever known—his quiet confidence belies a fierce and passionate patriotism. Robert H. Smith has demonstrated to me again and again the importance of quality in all things—his attention to detail is nothing short of amazing. I have tremendous respect for Richard Gilder and Lew Lehrman, who have used their corporate and political savvy to create a grassroots program that promotes history in the classroom. They are determined to make a difference, and their impact on teachers and students has been incredible. Jack Evans, the founder of Mount Vernon's volunteer program, still ranks as the most diplomatic and sensitive leader I have ever met. General Dave Palmer, former superintendent of West Point, is perhaps the best embodiment of character-driven leadership I have ever witnessed. Robert Budd Gibby's 50 years of work on behalf of George Washington provides a textbook case of leadership by example.

In my 23 years at Mount Vernon, I have worked with eight Regents—our charming name for the Chairman of the Board—and some 75 Vice Regents. Just as they span the different states in terms of their residences, their personalities have been tremendously varied as well. But they have all shared a deep commitment and enthusiasm for the two-fold mission of Mount Vernon—to preserve and to educate. They have been cautious one moment, brave the next—but their focus on Washington's legacy has never wavered.

Steve Spignesi's experience with so many books on so many different topics made him a very effective partner in the creation of this volume. He intuitively understood the most interesting aspects of Washington's personality, and how they would relate to the modern reader. Our agent, John White, served as a dependable and always encouraging bridge between us for the duration of the project, while Laurie Harting and her talented team at Wiley were a pleasure to work with from beginning to end.

Finally, I want to thank Kirk Blandford for his efforts to wean me away from the quill pen and introduce me to the wonders of computers. He was not entirely successful, but his patience and understanding was more than admirable.

James C. Rees
Mount Vernon, Virginia
October 1, 2006

STEPHEN SPIGNESI

*T*here are three people to whom I express enormous gratitude and give the most credit for this book:

The author, Mount Vernon Executive Director Jim Rees, an incredibly knowledgeable George Washington authority whose wise insights into Washington as both private man and influential leader made my job easier, and whose good and kind nature and boundless patience made him a pleasure personally to work with.

Our agent, John White, who believed in this book from the beginning, worked diligently to make it happen, and contributed to it in more ways than I can count.

John Wiley Senior Editor Laurie Harting, who was a joy to work with and whose advice and suggestions consistently made this book better.

Also, Wiley editor Micheline Frederick was a great help during the editing stages, and Anne Johnson at Mount Vernon and Wiley editor Mike Lewis also deserve singling out for their help and support. And, as always, my mother Lee, my wife Pam, and a few special friends (Renee, Domenica, Jennifer, Jim, and George in particular) have my deepest gratitude for their support.

It has been my honor to have worked with you all on such an uplifting and important book.

Stephen Spignesi
New Haven, Connecticut
October 1, 2006

Introduction
The Mark of a Leader

His was the singular destiny . . . of leading the armies of his country successfully through an arduous war for the establishment of its independence, of conducting its councils through the birth of a government, new in its forms and principles, until it settled down into a quiet and orderly train; and of scrupulously obeying the laws through the whole of his career, civil and military, of which the history of the world furnishes no other example.

—THOMAS JEFFERSON

The great difference between the real leader and the pretender is that the one sees into the future, while the other regards only the present; the one lives by the day, and acts upon expediency; the other acts on enduring principles and for the immortality.

—EDMUND BURKE

*W*ith all due respect to T.S. Eliot, it is December that is the cruelest month.

George Washington's five-hour ride on the grounds of Mount Vernon on December 12, 1799, a ride in which he was besieged by rain, sleet, and snow, certainly attests to the month's mean-spiritedness.

It would be Washington's last ride, because two days later he would be dead from a severely infected epiglottis. It was not a pleasant way to go—his airway gradually closed entirely—and Washington realized early on that the end was near. Minutes before he passed away, Washington asked his wife, Martha, to retrieve his two different last wills and testaments from his study. He selected one and had the other burned before his eyes. He was taking care of business in his usual fashion.

Not surprisingly, after fighting the infection for several hours, Washington exercised his authority as a leader— the leader of his own destiny—and instructed the three doctors present to allow him to die in peace. No more bleeding, no more purging, no more poultices.

He decided to surrender to Providence, that omnipresent, uncontrollable power that had humbled Washington all the days of his life.

His final words were, fittingly, instructional: "I am just going. Have me decently buried and do not let my body be put into a vault in less than two days after I am dead. Do you understand me? 'Tis well."

Washington was worried about being buried alive. Whispered stories of live interments were part and parcel of the period. Washington was, after all, a cautious and deliberate man who had conducted his research and used his good judgment. And his last words were, as usual, thoughtful and prudent.

Leadership is influencing people—by providing purpose, direction, and motivation—while operating

to accomplish the mission and improving the orga-
nization.

—*U.S. Army Handbook*[1]

Two important elements of effective leadership are confidence and trust.

Followers must have confidence in their leader's abilities, and they must have boundless trust in their leader's character and ethics.

Another factor, and one that is important when looking at George Washington as a leader, is *self*-confidence: the heartfelt faith that one's decisions are correct.

Leadership is a subtle power: hard to define, yet sometimes easy to recognize; a part of some people's nature, but also possible to nurture.

What makes a great leader?

What are the traits and characteristics of those history has defined as leaders?

Are people born with leadership skills? Not according to the great football coach Vince Lombardi, who said, "Leaders are made, they are not born. They are made by hard effort, which is the price which all of us must pay to achieve any goal that is worthwhile."

Leadership can be used for good (Washington, Nelson Mandela, et al.); it can be abused and used for nefarious purposes (Jim Jones, Osama bin Laden, et al.). The moral leader strives for great results. The amoral leader works for personal gain, regardless of the results.

Leadership is an ability, a skill. Sometimes people voluntarily agree to be led. They willingly follow the dictates of a charismatic leader. And sometimes people must obey a leader as a function of their position, their job, their place in a particular business or social dynamic. The point to keep in mind, however, is that the greatest leaders have the traits and skills to lead both of these groups, often simultaneously.

And many of these skills are definable, and can be cultivated by anyone aspiring to be an effective leader.

> *The heart of Washington's leadership was pure character. It sustained the troops at Valley Forge. It made the ratification of the Constitution possible. His character was defined by maturity and a capacity for growth.*
>
> —DAVID ABSHIRE[2]

A sterling character is really the combination of many well-honed traits. Some are talents people are born with; others are developed only through the trials of life. In the pages that follow, we will examine the specific traits that, when melded together, formulated the character of Washington.

A successful leader . . .

➤ Has a clear vision
➤ Is honest
➤ Is ambitious
➤ Is courageous
➤ Has self-control and discipline
➤ Takes responsibility
➤ Is determined
➤ Has a strong work ethic
➤ Uses good judgment
➤ Learns from mistakes
➤ Is humble
➤ Does the research
➤ Values presentation

➤ Exceeds expectations
➤ Has faith

Today, we are ravenous for effective leaders, but they seem incredibly hard to find. Our leaders regularly disappoint us; many shamelessly embrace self-indulgence. And among the rest of us—the followers, so to speak—apathy abounds.

The study of history proffers to all of us the examined lives of the long-past great, many of whom, flawed and insecure as they were, ultimately *set a standard.*

George Washington's leadership produced incredible results. His personal strength as a leader created a country. This can be said of no other American leader—and very few others in world history.

In *George Washington's Leadership Lessons,* we will look at all that made Washington who he was; we will touch upon the complex layers of Washington's character, all of which served to create a whole greater than the sum of its parts. Vision is nothing without ambition. Determination is nothing without courage.

George Washington was a very self-aware man, a man who labored to capitalize on his strengths and minimize his failings. Historian David McCullough said, "Washington wasn't chosen by his fellow members of the Continental Congress because he was a great military leader. He was chosen because they knew him; they knew the kind of man he was; they knew his character, his integrity.

"Washington was not, as were Adams, Jefferson, Franklin, and Hamilton, a learned man. He was not an intellectual. Nor was he a powerful speaker like his fellow Virginian Patrick Henry. What Washington was, above all, was a leader. He was a man people would follow."[3]

And he always led with a greater good in mind.

This is the mark of a leader whose legacy lives on.

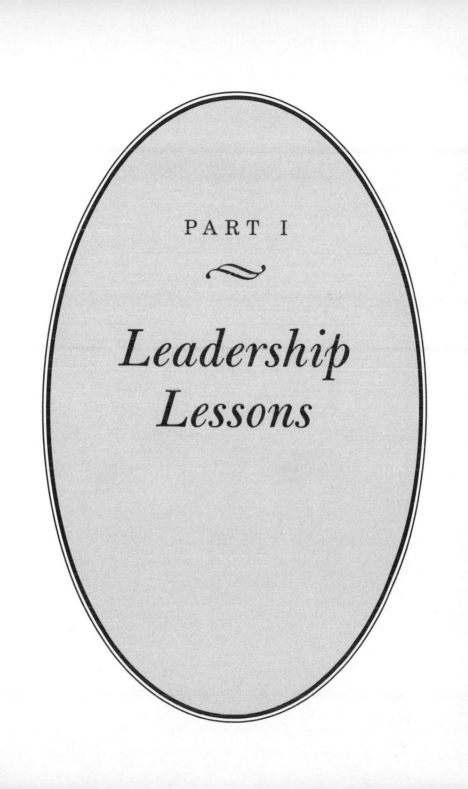

PART I

Leadership
Lessons

Leadership Lesson 1

~

A Leader Has Vision

The very essence of leadership is that you have to have a vision.

—THEODORE HESBURGH

*M*any Americans associate George Washington with strong and steady leadership. He bravely led the Continental Army in the War of Independence, and he then accepted the call to be first president of our new nation. But there was much more to Washington's leadership. In fact, very few people perceive of Washington as the creative, big-thinking, inspiring, visionary leader he actually was.

Reverend Richard C. Stazesky, in a February 2000 lecture at the George Washington Club in Wilmington, Delaware, discussed the three key traits of the "visionary leader"—he or she has a far-reaching view, is meticulously organized, and is personally persuasive.[1]

George Washington was a visionary leader of the highest degree, and his personal charisma and the staggeringly high level of respect and love felt for him were the tools he employed to implement his vision.

Perhaps Washington was fortunate (and we are even *more* fortunate) that he never visited Europe and also never completely understood the life of classic European nobility. Washington thought like an "American" before anyone actually knew what that really meant. He believed deeply in a republican form of government, and he similarly believed that what he described as our "great experiment" would really work. In a letter to Catherine Macaulay Graham, Washington wrote, "The establishment of our new Government seemed to be the last great experiment for promoting human happiness by reasonable compact in civil Society."[2]

He also understood that what we call a "free enterprise system"—emphasis on the word "free"—would be a powerful, motivational engine for our new country, a self-directed system that would provide new incentives for rapid growth. If properly nurtured, this system would reward Americans with higher and higher standards of living, as well as a greater sense of long-term security.

The Idea—and Ideal—of True Independence Washington's fundamental vision was of a United States free from foreign control. This idealized vision of a free America as put forth by Washington and the other Founders essentially established our cherished right to privacy. As Supreme Court Justice Louis Brandeis said two centuries later, "They conferred, as against the government, the right to be let alone—the most comprehensive of rights and the right most valued by civilized men."[3] This is the essence of big-picture thinking: As the colonies desired to be "let alone" by Britain, so individual Americans desired to be left alone by their government, to pursue wealth and happiness on their own terms. Washington recognized the practical side of this vision—that a central government would be necessary to hold the whole thing together—but he never lost sight of the importance of an overriding vision for a free America.

Putting a System in Place   Washington's willingness to serve as president of the 1787 Constitutional Convention in Philadelphia is evidence of his far-reaching understanding of the need for structure and organization. Ideals like those expressed in the Declaration of Independence were relatively easy to agree upon, but Washington understood the need to translate this vision into practical terms. He knew that one of the first rules of business is "get it in writing." In modern times, this may be a cliché, perhaps most frequently associated with used-car salespeople and some fast-talking real estate agents. But as is often the case with hoary old adages, this cliché boasts a great deal of truth. Washington knew that the only way for his new country to survive and prosper was to establish a clear set of written rules that all 13 states would agree to follow. He argued that compromises were essential, and he used his tremendous influence to force people to the bargaining table.

Interestingly, Washington wanted to remove some of the ambiguities that still exist today in the final document— that's the kind of detail-oriented thinker he was. Others recognized, however, that leaving some issues open to interpretation was a positive, not a negative, particularly in terms of the document's longevity. Washington was the first to admit that the written document formulated under his leadership was far from perfect—in his typical fashion, Washington wanted to keep people's expectations on a modest level. Still, this magnificent document has never been eclipsed as a road map for democracy. It has Washington's stamp on it—it's got vision, but it also works on a practical level.

Investing in an Uncertain Future   Washington ultimately acquired almost 70,000 acres of land in what would today be seven different states because he believed in America's future.

He did not know exactly how fast our nation would expand, nor did he know precisely in which direction growth would occur. But he was absolutely certain that America *would* expand, and he wanted to be at the forefront of this evolution by becoming a major landowner.

As an example of Washington's far-reaching thinking, in his will, he listed many parcels of his land, often emphasizing his belief in their future value. When talking about 373 acres in what would become the town of Nansemond, Virginia, he wrote that he had purchased the tracts "on full conviction that they would become valuable."[4] The acres were on a river that could facilitate commerce, and he described them as "capable of great improvement; and from its situation must become extremely valuable." Washington was thinking like a businessman, and he recognized that land would become America's second most important resource. In first place, of course, were our people—creative, hardworking, and eager to move forward.

Growth   The final pages of this book will reveal that Washington was an extraordinary farmer. He was constantly experimenting with crop rotations, improved equipment, and soil enhancements. He wholeheartedly believed that America's farmers would be the world's best, and that we would become "a storehouse and granary to the world."[5] And he was right.

Washington's Unavoidable Regret   As a slaveholder, Washington evolved morally to the point where he believed that slavery as an institution could not coexist with a true republican form of government. Hence, his long-term vision for America did not include slavery. He recognized its inhumanity, and even when his slaves were part and parcel of the operations of Mount Vernon, Washington's behavior illustrated his broader understanding of the regrettable institution. Washington once wrote to a visiting Englishman, "I can clearly foresee that nothing but the rooting out of slavery can perpetuate the existence of our union."[6]

Washington expressed an intuitive, heartfelt concern for his slaves and he worked diligently to treat them humanely. He made sure they were fed properly, recognized slave marriages, and was loath to break up slave families. Later in life, he stopped buying and selling slaves altogether. Although it took him quite a while to warm up to the idea, he saw to it that blacks served in the Continental Army. He scolded his overseers for thinking of slaves as "they do a draft horse or ox."[7] He enlisted doctors to treat the wounds and illnesses of his slaves. He allowed them to grow their own produce, which Washington sometimes purchased, and he trusted individual slaves to travel to nearby towns and plantations.[8]

As has been said many times, Washington's attitudes and actions regarding slavery must be judged within the context of his times, not ours. And for all his (oftentimes reluctant) acceptance of the institution, it is clear that he held in his heart a future vision of a time when slavery would be outlawed on American soil. He can be criticized for not making the elimination of slavery a presidential priority, although many scholars agree with Washington's opinion that the issue of slavery, if addressed head-on, would have destroyed the fragile Union. Given the choice between eliminating slavery or saving the Union, Washington really was between a rock and a hard place. He probably felt he had no choice—he picked the Union.

The First "Mr. President" "I walk on untrodden ground," Washington wrote to Catherine Macaulay Graham on January 9, 1790. "There is scarcely any part of my conduct which may not hereafter be drawn into precedent."[9]

Washington instinctively understood that everything he did as president was monumental in its long-term significance and meaning. With every act, he was establishing traditions and precedents for the future, so he always attempted to act "presidential."

He fully recognized the importance and weight of the presidency, and he knew that future presidents would look to his deeds and words for inspiration and guidance. "Many things which appear of little importance in themselves," Washington wrote to John Jay, Hamilton, Madison, and John Adams shortly after his inauguration "may have great and durable consequences from their having been established at the commencement of a new general government."[10]

By refusing a third term, Washington looked ahead to the future of our government and insisted on the peaceful transfer of power to a new generation of leaders. By doing so, not only did he follow through on his promise to the people, he also ensured that our future leaders would be chosen on merit—rather than on bloodlines or military rank. They would truly be chosen by the people. Washington trusted the people and the system, and he envisioned a nation that could fulfill a greater promise and potential than any nation in history.

Designing for the Future   Washington helped to select the site for our nation's capital, and he enlisted a very creative and controversial architect—Pierre L'Enfant—who shared with Washington a "think big and bold" approach to the design of the city. In his mind, Washington was creating a capital that would last for centuries, not decades, and the city he envisioned was destined to be world class. Washington outmaneuvered the naysayers (including Thomas Jefferson) who felt the plans were far too grandiose, far too reminiscent of the royal courts of Europe. As the National Register of Historic Places explains on its web site, "In the context of the United

States, a plan as grand as the 200-year old city of Washington, DC, stands alone in its magnificence and scale. But as the capital of a new nation, its position and appearance had to surpass the social, economic and cultural balance of a mere city: it was intended as the model for American city planning and a symbol of governmental power to be seen by other nations. The remarkable aspect of Washington, is that by definition of built-out blocks and unobstructed open space, the plan conceived by L'Enfant is little changed today."[11] This is a testimony to Washington's vision—and the fact that he had the power and influence to back it up.

At Home George Washington's architecture at Mount Vernon boasts elegant, classical themes, but it is also fresh and full of new ideas. For his beloved home, Washington embraced and incorporated elements that were distinctly American, ultimately creating a hybrid design that honors the past while looking to the future.

Leadership Lesson 2

~

A Leader Is Honest

I hope I shall always possess firmness and virtue enough to maintain (what I consider the most enviable of all titles) the character of an honest man.

— GEORGE WASHINGTON[1]

*G*eorge Washington truly believed that only an honest man could sustain an unblemished reputation. The cherry tree story, though known to be a panegyric fabrication by Parson Weems, clearly illustrates Washington's lifelong devotion to an honest lifestyle, so it's worth retelling to each new generation.

Consistent honesty is a key ingredient of character, and Washington believed that you had to be good before you could be great. And he was unwavering in his insistence on the glorious nobility and timeless value of unimpeachable truth. "I hold the maxim no less applicable to public than to private affairs," he wrote, "that honesty is always the best policy."[2]

Like Money in the Bank This reputation for honesty was especially vital during the Revolutionary War, when Washington faced a string of losses that would have destroyed the careers of most soldiers. Several of his officers and a number of civilian leaders began to question his talents as a general and his judgment as a leader. But no one dared to question his honesty. He could not be corrupted, and his standards could not be compromised.

On Orders from the General   Like the best CEOs, Washington believed in speaking and acting with clocklike consistency and in communicating unwavering ethical tenets to his officers and troops. If Washington said something to his men, they could depend upon it to be true.

For instance, Washington would not allow his hungry soldiers to raid farms during the Revolutionary War—stealing was stealing; it was as simple as that. He also knew that if his army alienated average citizens, they would be much more tempted to side with the Crown. In 1777, during the Battle of Brandywine in Pennsylvania, General Washington issued specific orders prohibiting looting; the British commander, William Howe, felt no such compunction, and his troops ultimately confiscated thousands of dollars of food and supplies from the mostly Quaker residents of Chadds Ford.

This was not an afterthought for Washington. As early as 1755, when he was still in his 20s, he was insisting upon steadfast honesty from his men, as ordered in the following letter to Robert Spotswood:

> You are hereby ordered, as soon as the Clothes and Arms arrive, to furnish all the men who now Rendezvous at Fredericksburgh, with both; and march them immediately with the utmost dispatch to Fort Cumberland, to reinforce the Garrison. When you arrive at Winchester, you must provide your men with Cartridges. You are to be very careful and

circumspect in your march; and see that your men do not on any account whatsoever, plunder or pillage the Houses which the people have deserted, or any others, or Plantations.[3]

Washington was very clear about his revulsion for soldiers who wantonly plundered and destroyed property, likening them to nothing more than a mob: "The distinction between a well regulated Army, and a Mob, is the good order and discipline of the first, and the licentious and disorderly behaviour of the latter."[4]

Corporate policy is corporate policy, and a strong, consistent top-down message—a message that advocates honesty in all dealings with outside constituents—benefits not only the team, but the entire corporation.

By the Book When Benedict Arnold turned traitor and attempted to turn West Point over to the British, Washington was crushed by the betrayal. Although Arnold escaped, Washington's men managed to capture British commander George Clinton's go-between, Major John André, who was found guilty of being a spy and sentenced to death. According to military tradition, because André was an officer, he was entitled to execution by firing squad. But Washington broke with this tradition. His established policy was to hang traitors, regardless of their standing in the military. In this case, remaining consistent with his own rules was simply more important to Washington than an old-world tradition. Washington ordered André hung on October 2, 1780, even though many of the commander in chief's own advisors had cautioned him that it was a bad public relations move.

The lesson for business leaders? Strict adherence to policy establishes a foundation of consistency and a corporate reputation for dependability. Washington almost never wavered; today, it is even more critical that the words and actions of business leaders sustain a positive perception of their company.

The Whole Truth, and Nothing But   Washington wrote some 20,000 individual letters, and it's hard to find a lie—more than that of flattering a friend who didn't deserve the compliment—in a single missive.

In addition to maintaining a passionate devotion to the truth in his correspondences, Washington was also a fervent protector of his own reputation for honesty, as evidenced by his September 17, 1757, letter to Virginia Lieutenant Governor Robert Dinwiddie, in which he states his anger at a rumor circulating that he had acted indecorously and against the lieutenant governor's wishes.

George Washington was, in a word, *furious:* "[N]o man, that ever was employed in a public capacity, has endeavoured to discharge the trust reposed in him with greater honesty, and more zeal for the country's interest, than I have done; and if there is any person living, who can say with justice, that I have offered any intentional wrong to the public, I will cheerfully submit to the most ignominious punishment, that an injured people ought to inflict."[5]

Throughout his life, Washington was fairly thin-skinned in response to criticism. As the years passed, he became accustomed to the fact that people would sometimes disagree with his decisions. But what he *never* understood was how anyone could criticize his motives, because he worked so diligently to remain honorable, regardless of the circumstances.

As prolific as he was with a quill pen, Washington became an amazingly careful communicator later in life. He chose his words wisely and seldom assumed that anything in writing would remain private.

Today, e-mails have supplanted letters as the preferred form of communication in many business interactions. And unlike letters, which seem to foster a certain formality in tone and form, e-mails are often an odd hybrid of a quick note and hasty phone call. Although the form is still evolving, the casualness and ease with which e-mails can be written can sometimes result in messages being misunderstood. Because grammatical and spelling errors are deemed more acceptable in e-mail communications, there is a tendency to avoid reviewing or proofreading the text. Mistakes slip by more easily.

Strict adherence to accuracy, no matter what the form of communication, prevents misunderstandings and unfortunate business consequences.

Honesty Translates into Trust It was a surprise to absolutely no one when Washington was tapped to be the president of the Constitutional Convention, because the other delegates knew that only Washington could pull people together. Why? Because the people trusted Washington. His popularity transcended geographical boundaries and class distinction. After all, he was a true-blue southerner, but northerners loved him because he had pushed the enemy out of Boston and New York during the Revolutionary War. He was beloved by fellow farmers and merchants, by the rich and the poor, by the young and the old.

That's why he had the power, the authority, to shut the doors of the convention hall and say, unequivocally, we *will* work together, and we *will* make compromises, because what is at stake is a new order, a government truly by the people and for the people. And in crafting the Constitution, the authors created a new office called the *presidency* for one specific man. When Supreme Court Justice Anthony Kennedy spoke at Mount Vernon on George Washington's birthday a few years ago, he explained that Washington was *his* hero. Because, if you study the Constitution, you'll see page after page of direction to the legislative branch, and quite a bit of direction to the judicial branch, but very, very little about the most powerful position of all, the presidency. That's because everyone trusted George Washington to make the rules, to set the precedents once he assumed the job. It was an awesome responsibility, and Washington, once again, rose to the occasion.

I once heard a famous corporate executive declare, "You don't earn power, or ask for power, you take it." Washington's life defies this Machiavellian approach to leadership. Washington did not grab power—he simply waited on the sidelines until the people recognized his supreme leadership and presented power to him willingly, even eagerly.

Counterpoint: *All Is Fair*

Knowledge Is Power

George Washington is often referred to as America's first spymaster, because he believed that a strong intelligence network was essential to winning the Revolutionary War.

In 1778, Washington ordered the creation of the Culper Ring, an undercover organization whose mission was to infiltrate the British in New York City and transmit information about their plans and activities—ship arrivals and departures, troop movements, the status of ammunition and supplies—back to General Washington in New Jersey. Among the tactics the Culper Ring employed were double agents, disappearing ink, and coded letters. Getting such intelligence to Washington would seem like a simple task—New Jersey is, after all, quite close to New York. A short trip in a southwesterly direction is all it should have taken to bring the general the intelligence he needed.

But such expediency had to be sacrificed for safety. That's why any news destined for the eyes of General Washington traveled a circuitous route from New York City to Long Island, across the Sound, into Fairfield on the Connecticut coast, and then overland to Washington's New Jersey headquarters.

Many of the secret messages were written using a special invisible ink known as Sympathetic Stain, created by James Jay, a doctor who lived in England. To the casual observer, the missives looked like nothing more than blank sheets of paper. But General Washington had in his possession a special liquid that, when brushed onto the blank paper, made the words appear. (More sophisticated agents would sometimes use invisible ink between the lines of an existing letter.) The most important people and places had their own special ciphers:

"711" meant *General Washington; "727"* meant *New York; "161"* meant *September; "178"* meant *the enemy;* and *"317"* meant *importance.*
"745" meant *England;* and *"680"* stood for *war.*

To further disguise messages, none of the letters of the alphabet stood for themselves; instead, they were all part of a substitute cipher. For instance, "a, b, c, d" meant *g, h, i, j.*

The secret code added another layer of security to the correspondences of the Culper Ring, which proved to be a great success.

The Culper Spy Ring Route

1. After gathering information about the British in New York, **Robert Townsend** (aka Samuel Culper, Jr.) would clandestinely pass the intelligence to Austin Roe (aka Agent 724), who was conveniently (i.e., *deliberately*) in the city to gather supplies.

2. **Austin Roe** would then head for his saloon, Roe's Tavern, in Setauket, Long Island, stopping along the way at Abraham Woodhull's farm (Woodhull was known as Samuel Culper, Sr.), to leave a message indicating that there was information to be transmitted.

3. **Abraham Woodhull** would then signal his neighbor **Anna Smith Strong** (aka Nancy Smith, but probably

referred to only as Agent 355, which stood for "lady") to send a message to Caleb Brewster (aka Agent 725) that Woodhull needed to meet with him. She would do so by hanging a black petticoat on her clothesline, along with a number of white handkerchiefs to communicate the hour of the meeting.

4. **Caleb Brewster** would then meet with Abraham Woodhull, accept the information for General Washington, and convey it across Long Island Sound on his whaleboat.

5. Brewster would then hand off the information to a select group of covert couriers, who would take it to **Benjamin Tallmadge** (aka John Bolton), who was often stationed in Fairfield, Connecticut.

6. Tallmadge would then discreetly travel to New Windsor, where he would personally hand the intelligence to **General George Washington** (aka 711).

The British never learned of the Culper Ring's existence. But many members of the ring were fully aware that there were British spies in their midst, and that their lives were always on the line. In fact, one early Culper Ring operative was Nathan Hale, who had only one life to lose for his country.

In summation, it is clear that Washington knew how to be deceitful in war, where the rules of civility were overruled by the adage "All is fair in love and war."[6, 7, 8]

Leadership Lesson 3

~

A Leader Has Ambition

It should be the highest ambition of every American to extend his views beyond himself, and to bear in mind that his conduct will not only affect himself, his country, and his immediate posterity; but that its influence may be co-extensive with the world, and stamp political happiness or misery on ages yet unborn.

—GEORGE WASHINGTON[1]

*G*eorge Washington was one of the most overtly ambitious young men in American history. He was bold and aggressive in his efforts to climb the ladder—in fact, *many* ladders—political, social, financial, military, and others, to the highest echelon.

What makes Washington special in this regard is that he established clear-cut priorities. He aspired to great *honor*, not great fortune, although he was resolute in his pursuit of financial rewards as well. Washington felt he would attain this honor through remarkable accomplishments and service to his nation. Particularly as a young man, Washington unapologetically craved the fame that came with such honor, although he maintained a sincere modesty that most celebrities and politicians today would find inconceivable. Washington was something of a paradox: He manifested ambition and humility at the same time, a sensibility which many who crave greatness are incapable of summoning.

Following the Rules   As a teenager, Washington aspired to the traits and behaviors called *civility*, defined in *Encarta* as a "formal politeness that results from observing social conventions."

Thus, when he was introduced to what have come to be known as the *Rules of Civility*, a Jesuit compilation of instructions on how to behave with courtesy and morality, he took the time to copy the rules by hand into his notebook, a practice commonly used at the time to encourage both penmanship and memorization. But Washington took the assignment far more seriously. Barely 16, he already seemed to understand that the first five letters of "civilization" formed the word "civil." He knew that he needed to work to achieve the standards of elevated behavior appropriate to a respected and worthy man.

The Value of Networking   After the death of his father, Augustine, and under the tutelage of his older brother, Washington embraced wholeheartedly the notion of becoming a "gentleman," an important credential for all white males destined to assume leadership positions. He excelled in fencing and became as comfortable on a horse as he was in a chair. His wide-ranging reading supported his cultural interests, and he began to assemble an impressive library.

But he also recognized the importance of social graces like dancing. In fact, he paid for his own dance lessons so he would be competent and *confident* on the dance floor.

As noted by historian Edward Lengel, "Dancing grew to become one of Washington's favorite pastimes, and his skill in the ballroom, and in pleasant conversation at the table, made him a welcome guest in the homes of politically influential neighbors."[2]

A timely parallel to Washington's ambitious striving for societal, cultural, and economic acceptance is the always-effective tactic of networking. The *Wall Street Journal*'s executive career web site, careerjournal.com, defines networking as "using shared interests to develop and maintain mutually beneficial relationships." This is precisely the course that Washington instinctively knew to take.

There is an old adage that boasts an epic truth: People like to work with people they like. And an important corollary to that adage is that people like others who like what they like. Washington understood this. He made sure he was competent in the fields of interest that all the "right people" were most passionate about.

The Importance of Friends   Patronage in Washington's time was critically important, and Washington, even at a young age, knew that the death of his father had left him, in a sense, floundering socially and in need of wealthy, influential, connected friends.

Washington was fortunate in that he soon acquired a familial connection to the socially prominent Fairfax family when his older half-brother Lawrence married Anne Fairfax. We also know that patriarch William Fairfax was especially fond of George and treated him almost like a son.

The Fairfaxes, whom historian Joseph Ellis describes as "the supreme example of privileged bloodlines [and] royal patronage,"[3] introduced Washington to a new, far more prominent social circle at their Belvoir estate.

Letitia Baldrige, in her introduction to Mount Vernon's edition of the *Rules of Civility,* explains, "As a frequent visitor [to Belvoir], he learned to comport himself with ease among the rich and titled visitors from England and Europe. It was a totally different milieu from his childhood, one that provided him not only with enjoyment, but also with learning, polish and great political opportunities."[4]

Mapping a Future   Once he recognized that his family circumstances would not allow him to attend college, Washington climbed very rapidly in the surveying ranks. Always enamored of maps and meticulous about their accuracy, Washington sketched sample survey maps in his school workbooks and did land surveys when he was barely 16. Washington's association with the Fairfax family led to his introduction to the formal profession of surveying, which combined Washington's natural attention to detail, his acumen in mathematics, and his love of the great outdoors.

After accompanying George William Fairfax on a surveying trip across the Blue Ridge Mountains in 1748 (which he chronicled in a small notebook as "Journey Over the Mountains"), Washington decided to throw all of his energy into becoming the best surveyor he possibly could. A year later, he was appointed county surveyor for Culpeper, Virginia, an important job with a great deal of responsibility for a lad of 17. For the next three years, his earnings—sometimes more than 100 pounds a year—rivaled those of area lawyers.[5]

What this episode of Washington's life demonstrates is that good leaders grab opportunities as they come—"they take the cookies when they're passed," as Mount Vernon's chairman of the board, Gay Hart Gaines, likes to say. They don't let their lack of funds, education, or standing in society prevent them from achieving a high level of success. Good leaders use their existing connections, and perhaps more important, they aggressively seek new connections. They don't wait around for lightning to strike.

First to Volunteer   Washington's ambition, combined with the Fairfax family's patronage, presented the 21-year-old

Washington with an opportunity for which he, at first glance, would seem wholly unsuited.

Royal Lieutenant Governor Robert Dinwiddie had been instructed by Great Britain to respectfully *request* the French to remove themselves from the Ohio Valley west of the Allegheny Mountains, land both the British and the French laid claim to. If this polite overture was rebuffed by the French, Dinwiddie was given the go-ahead to "drive them off by Force of Arms."[6]

Washington's patron, William Fairfax, who was an advisor to the governor, informed Washington of the risky mission. Almost immediately, Washington eagerly volunteered to make his way through the wilderness to the French stronghold. In all likelihood, Washington faced little competition for the job—the mission was not just dangerous, but time-sensitive. If he failed to travel quickly and without incident, winter weather would make the trip all the more hazardous. The governor was probably skeptical about giving such an important task to such a young man; nevertheless, Washington talked his way into a job. As historian Peter Henriques notes, "George Washington's appointment as Dinwiddie's emissary was one of the truly determining moments of his life."[7]

Ultimately, the mission itself was a failure. The French refused to budge—and the French and Indian War ultimately decided the question of which nation owned the Ohio Valley. But what mattered to young Washington was that he had stepped up when opportunity arose. His willingness to serve set the stage for him to climb the military ladder at a very rapid pace.

Washington's advancement in the Virginia Militia during the French and Indian War resulted in a commission as colonel at the remarkable age of 23. He was already one of the most talked-about military men in the colonies, and the journals he wrote to describe the mission became hot properties, even in England and France.

Marrying Up   When Daniel Custis died in 1757, he left his 26-year-old wife, Martha, an estate that would today have made her a millionaire many times over.

Three plantations totaling 4,000 acres, 85 slaves, 324 head of cattle, 225 hogs, 97 sheep, and a gristmill were under the immediate and sole authority of Martha, instantly elevating her to the highest echelon of Virginia society. It is difficult to be absolutely certain, but in all probability, Martha Custis was probably the wealthiest widow in Virginia, and certainly one of the wealthiest in the colonies.

Did George Washington marry Martha for her money? Her wealth certainly played a role in his thinking, as discussed by Peter Henriques in *Realistic Visionary:*

> George Washington's marriage to Martha Dandridge Custis was to a significant degree a marriage of convenience. However, it should be emphasized that it was a marriage of convenience for both of them.[8]

From Martha's point of view, George Washington was an established war hero, as well as a tall and handsome Virginia gentleman. He owned a plantation in a beautiful area of Virginia, and his recent election to the House of Burgesses reflected his prominent status in the community. From all accounts, he would make a good father to her two children.

Despite Martha's matronly appearance in surviving portraits, she was known as an attractive and personable young widow, with a good head for business. But her bank account was equally important, as Henriques notes:

> Martha's wealth was undoubtedly a major attraction to George Washington. There is no question he hoped to marry a wealthy woman, as he had tried to do so unsuccessfully in the past. It is probably safe to assert

that he would not have married Martha if she had not been wealthy.[9]

But this was not the crass, self-seeking move it may appear to be to our twenty-first-century sensibilities. This is often *how it was done* in eighteenth-century Virginia. Marriages were unashamedly and forthrightly business transactions as well as romantic unions. Families joined, estates expanded, wealth increased—it was the circle of life for the landed gentry. George Washington was, after all, a man of his time. Thus, his marriage to Martha was an ambitious move—for both husband and wife.

Ultimately, a deep and lasting love grew between George and Martha, and their loyalty and commitment to each other was profound and undeniable. Not all leaders, of course, are fortunate enough to marry for both love and money. But the most important lesson to be learned is that Washington treated this decision with great care and concern, and that his commitment to the marriage was strong and enduring.

After her husband died in the bed they had shared for so long, Martha never slept there again. She abandoned the master bedroom and moved to the third floor of the Mansion, where she slept for the last two-and-a-half years of her life.

Leadership Lesson 4

~

A Leader Is Courageous

Courage is going from failure to failure without losing enthusiasm.

—WINSTON CHURCHILL

No single individual in American history so boldly and frequently risked his own life for the good of the cause. America is a reality because of one man's courage.

Washington's near-death experiences included battles with Mother Nature, the fiercest actions of war, and the ravages of disease—and he came through them all virtually unscathed. But Washington's dauntless courage was also expressed in his willingness to accept so many challenges that would have intimidated the average man. He possessed the courage of his convictions, and he was brave for all the right reasons.

We can wonder today what would have happened if Washington had fallen during the many skirmishes, battles, and ailments he ultimately survived. Was his courage foolhardy? Was he reckless in his willingness to accept risks, or was his courage simply a sign of stalwart, heroic bravery manifested in time of peril?

Perhaps the answers to these questions are irrelevant,

since whatever risks Washington accepted were ultimately overcome. It is instructive, however, in light of Washington's historical importance, to consider the immediate and un-wavering eagerness with which Washington forged ahead against all odds, certainly not unaware of the risks, but accepting and sometimes joyfully unafraid of them. This is courage in the raw—an intuitive, visceral bravery that is hard for most people to imagine.

Treachery and Ice   In the fall of 1753, Washington was given a special assignment by the royal governor. He was to travel to an encampment south of Lake Erie and warn the French to forsake all claims to the Ohio Valley—or else. Still unversed in the tactics of diplomacy and strategic intercourse, Washington was quickly rebuffed by the French, who vir-tually ignored the governor's request. With winter fast approaching, Washington and his guide, Christopher Gist, a fur trader with a middling ability to understand French, knew they had to make exceptionally good time on the return trip. But it was already too late—heavy snow and a lack of food caused the pair to abandon their horses and travel on foot.

Washington's diaries tell the story of a remarkable jour-ney that included two death-defying experiences. The first was the result of a betrayal; the second, the cruel vagaries of the wilderness in the winter.

At an Indian village called Murthering Town, Washington accepted the assistance of an Indian guide who promised to show them a shortcut through the woods. Gist did not trust this Indian guide, but Washington insisted they needed his help. Unfortunately, the more experienced Gist acquiesced to the strong will of the younger man.

The Indian guide led them through the woods, seemingly without incident. But then, when they reached a clearing, the

Indian suddenly ran ahead. He turned and fired at Washington and Gist, fortuitously missing both men, despite the close range. The two surprised men reacted quickly—they overwhelmed and captured the Indian, but ultimately let him go. Gist had wanted to execute him, but Washington refused to allow it.

Two days after the shooting incident, Washington and Gist faced their second crisis: The Allegheny River, which they needed to cross, was almost completely impassable due to huge chunks of floating ice. But with no viable choice remaining, they decided to attempt a crossing on a makeshift raft.

As soon as the raft was in the river, however, it was pummeled and trapped by the floating ice. Washington, trying to keep the raft afloat, fell overboard. He scrambled his way back onto the raft, but it soon fell apart. The two men struggled to reach a small island in the middle of the river.

We can only imagine the misery the two nearly frozen men endured that night, knowing that they were trapped on an island and probably doomed to freeze to death. But they survived the night and awoke to the sight of a completely frozen, now-traversable river. Washington ultimately made it back to Virginia, and his journal account of his courageous mission to the French encampment was first published in the *Maryland Gazette* in March 1754. With typical Washingtonian modesty, his account began:

> As it was thought advisable by his Honour the Governor to have the following account of my Proceedings to and from the French on Ohio, committed to print; I think I can do no less than apologize, in some Measure, for the numberless Imperfections of it.[1]

But Washington's modesty did not prevent him from describing his exploits in very dramatic and heroic terms—he knew the value of a strong public relations campaign.

His bravery and determination immediately elevated young Washington's reputation and standing to a national level—and it remained there until his death.

Courage and Caution As a young colonel, George Washington was absolutely fearless in battle. In fact, his over-confidence sometimes caused him to become downright cocky. On May 31, 1754, Washington's Virginia Regiment attacked a small force of French soldiers on a diplomatic mission—a serious and deadly departure from established military protocol. To say the least, this was not a shining moment in Washington's still-young career. In fact, this attack is now considered the battle that began the French and Indian War.

Following his first taste of being fired upon, Washington wrote, "I can with truth assure you, I heard Bullets whistle and believe me there was something charming in the sound."[2] It is said that King George II, upon hearing of Washington's statement, remarked, "He would not say so, if he had been used to hear many."[3] In essence, the king was poking fun at Washington's youthful enthusiasm for war, and predicting, quite correctly, that it wouldn't last.

In 1897, perhaps in homage to Washington's immortal line, Winston Churchill wrote in *The Story of the Malakand Field Force,* "Nothing in life is so exhilarating as to be shot at without result."[4] In other words, nothing is more exciting than a near miss.

But Washington's lust for the battlefield did not last. By the end of the revolution, his words reflected a deep and abiding respect for peace. He also selected a dove of peace weathervane to crown his home. Fortunately, Washington was a leader who performed equally well in both arenas—war and peace. His knowledge of the former helped him to be a more effective leader in the latter.

Taking Charge   During the Battle of Monmouth in 1778, General Charles Lee, George Washington's second in command, ordered Continental troops to retreat, believing they had no chance against the larger British forces.

As they retreated, they came upon none other than General Washington himself, who was furious at Lee's incompetence and ineffective judgments. Making an immediate decision to countermand Lee's orders and engage the British, Washington rushed to the front of the lines to rally and instruct the men. The battle was a technical draw, but it proved that Washington was relentless and stunningly brave when he was required to seize an opportunity.

Later, Lee was shameless in his self-aggrandizement and lambasting of Washington. In a letter to Robert Morris, he wrote, "By all that's sacred, General Washington had scarcely any more to do [in the Battle of Monmouth] than to strip the dead."[5] Lee boasted that he had been the one to manifest "great presence of mind" and maneuver the British "from their advantageous into as disadvantageous a one."[6] All of which, of course, was pure poppycock. Figuring that the best defense was a good offense, Lee demanded a trial to argue his point. This turned out to be a foolhardy move, since he was found guilty of disrespect, disobeying orders, and other offenses. He was removed from duty for a period of one year.[7]

Victory above All   Washington's unexpected defeat of the British at Trenton and Princeton showed leadership bolstered by unwavering bravery and courage. It took a tremendous amount of self-confidence to cross the Delaware River. To make such a move when the odds were so heavily stacked against him, combined with the fact that he and his men had already suffered a number of humiliating defeats, is the mark of a stalwart leader who puts victory above all.

Militarily, the victories at Trenton and Princeton were fairly insignificant. But the political and psychological benefits of such an embarrassing defeat of the British rallied public support. Rampant discouragement among Washington's troops was replaced with hope and encouragement.

Leadership Lesson 5

~

A Leader Has Self-Control

Remember not only to say the right thing in the right place, but far more difficult still, to leave unsaid the wrong thing at the tempting moment.

—BENJAMIN FRANKLIN

Prudent, cautious self-control is wisdom's root.

—ROBERT BURNS

$\mathcal{A}$ s part of the never-ending study of "The Father of Our Country," historians and scholars have long pointed out that the evolution of Washington into the nation's greatest hero was something Washington himself was quite conscious of—he maintained maximum control of his actions and his reputation in order to achieve this greatness without distasteful self-promotion.

Washington understood the existence of—and the need for—the Washington *persona,* an idealized, exemplary father figure and leader who held to the highest standards, and who always put the good of the country—and its people—over his own needs, wants, and interests.

Washington was known for his dignity under every circumstance. He believed in moderation in all things, and he practiced what he preached.

Always in Moderation   George and Martha Washington entertained almost constantly at Mount Vernon, and we know that in the year 1798 they hosted at least 677 overnight guests. Wine and liquor were typically served at the main meal, and Washington almost always partook. But it would seem that he was careful never to drink to excess—there is not a single reference to Washington acting even mildly tipsy. The same can be said for Washington's dining habits—he loved good food but was never a glutton. He seldom used tobacco, and he treated the opposite sex with a level of respect and admiration that many of his peers did not share.

In essence, Washington never lost control of his own behavior, and his moderation in all things never gave his critics an easy target. Washington knew that his leadership could be compromised by the smallest of errors.

Weighing Consequences   Washington understood that his fiery temper, if left unchecked, could be his downfall and completely undermine his ability to lead. As historian Richard Brookhiser explains, "[Washington's] form was imposing, and his temper was dangerous. Displaying the one, and controlling the other, was essential to his success as a leader."[1]

Did George Washington read Confucius? And if he did, might he have come across one particular bit of wisdom from the sage philosopher in which he advised, "When anger rises, think of the consequences"? Regardless of how Washington developed this particular practice, we know he clearly employed its tenets. Washington thought things through and reined in his temper when he recognized he was allowing his emotions to run away with him. The Australian polio pioneer Elizabeth Kenny once said, "He who angers you, conquers you." Washington was verily *living* this edict. And he knew that if he allowed his anger to give an advantage to those who wished to extinguish the fight for liberty, all would be lost. This wise restraint is the essence of directed self-control.

Staying above the Fray   During his presidency, members of Washington's own cabinet were less than loyal—particularly Thomas Jefferson. Yet Washington was rarely vengeful, in words or deeds. For the most part, he kept his feelings under emotional lock and key.

We know that Thomas Jefferson was livid that Washington followed advice provided by Alexander Hamilton. Jefferson, while a member of Washington's administration, essentially made it possible for the writer Philip Freneau to establish the *National Gazette,* a vocal, anti-administration newspaper. This blatant and deliberate undermining of the administration was a personal betrayal of the first order. In fact, the great Washington biographer Douglas Southall Freeman described Jefferson as "little short of being a fiend" in terms of his involvement with Freneau.[2]

Historian Emory B. Elliot, Jr., writing in *The Princeton Companion,* concluded that "Freneau's *National Gazette* upheld Jefferson's 'Republican' principles and even condemned Washington's foreign policy. Jefferson later praised Freneau for having 'saved our Constitution which was galloping fast into monarchy.' "[3]

Washington was well aware of Jefferson's involvement with Freneau and also of what was being written about him in the *National Gazette.* But did he rant and rave, and demean himself by a mounting a counterattack?

Hardly. When pressed, Washington referred to the editor as "that rascal Freneau."[4] Under the circumstances, this was an incredibly reserved response—Washington simply refused to enter the fray.

Jefferson was by no means the only leader who used the media to play politics, yet it is Washington who was atypical, who set himself apart—he hated party politics and all they entailed.[5]

Washington was incredibly sensitive to criticism, and he disliked the press with as much passion as many modern presidents. For example, in his March 1790 letter to David Stuart, Washington described newspapermen as "stuffing their papers with scurrility and nonsensical declamation"[6] Yet what is most notable about Washington is that he expressed most of his frustration in private, not public: He held back. He maintained a dignity and an "above it all" status that secured his unique position on a higher pedestal.

What the Heart Wants   While in his 20s, Washington fell in love with Sally Fairfax, the wife of his friend and neighbor George Fairfax. In a letter to Sally, written in the fall of 1758, while Washington was recovering from yet another bout of dysentery, he professed himself a "votary to Love." He wrote, "You have drawn me . . . into an honest confession of a Simple Fact. . . . The world has no business to know the object of my love, declared in this manner to—you, when I want to conceal it."[7]

For both Washington and, ultimately, our nation, this could have been a catastrophic situation. He had close personal and professional ties with George Fairfax, plus he was engaged to Martha Custis at the time he wrote the letters.

But the situation itself was extremely tempting. George Fairfax was traveling in England, while George Washington was recovering from an illness with the help of an eighteenth-century-style candy striper, none other than Sally Fairfax.

Still, in all likelihood, Washington never surrendered to the wants of his heart. At least in public—who will ever know for sure what happened in private?—Washington maintained a strict decorum in his dealings with another man's wife. Washington did indeed marry Martha, and he nurtured a strong and lasting relationship with the Fairfax family for years to come.

(Note: Washington's "love letter," which Sally Fairfax saved for 50 years, was discovered only after her death. It is now archived at Harvard University.)

There is an important business lesson here: Calling upon deliberate self-control, Washington sublimated his emotional wants for *multiple* greater goods. He knew that if he had acted on his desires, his business dealings with the most important family in Virginia would have ended. His impending marriage to Martha Custis would have been placed at risk, and his reputation as a man of honor would have been sullied, perhaps beyond redemption. The bottom line is that Washington's self-control enabled his integrity to remain intact.

History abounds with stories of men—in both business and personal situations—who abandoned virtuous self-control and were subsequently dealt tragic consequences.[8]

Counterpoint: Justifiable Rage?

As we have seen, Washington was known for having a bad temper that he almost never lost. He aspired to total control of his emotions, and, for the most part, he succeeded.

But there were exceptions. A fellow officer once reported (perhaps apocryphally) that Washington raged at General

Charles Lee at the Battle of Monmouth in a particularly animated manner: "He swore 'til the leaves shook on the trees. Never in my life have I heard such wonderful swearing."[8]

An interesting counterpoint to this incident is that Washington proclaimed during the war that cursing was banned among his soldiers!

On August 3, 1776, Washington issued a General Order, which stated:

> The General is sorry to be informed that the foolish and wicked practice of profane cursing and swearing, a vice heretofore little known in an American army, is growing into fashion. He hopes the officers will, by example as well as influence, endeavor to check it, and that both they and the men will reflect, that we can have little hope of the blessing of Heaven on our arms, if we insult it by our impiety and folly. Added to this, it is a vice so mean and low, without any temptation, that every man of sense and character detests and despises it.[9]

Interestingly, Washington started with an appeal to his soldiers' religious sensibilities, and then reminded them that men of good character always refrain from swearing.

Leadership Lesson 6

~

A Leader Takes
Personal Responsibility

The ability to accept responsibility is the measure of the man.

—ROY L. SMITH

The price of greatness is responsibility.

—WINSTON CHURCHILL

The great English playwright Tom Stoppard once said that "responsibilities gravitate to the person who can shoulder them."

It is difficult for modern Americans to fully understand the risks and sacrifices that Washington and the other Founders willingly accepted in order to mount a successful revolution. Today, a common perception of this epic struggle is that of a unified rebellion sweeping across 13 colonies with great spirit and boundless enthusiasm; a boisterous time of skirmishes, raids, and rallying cries during which most, if not all, of the period's stalwart citizenry were active participants in the noble cause.

The reality is far less inspiring. Even well after the war had begun, only about a fourth of the colonists were committed revolutionaries, and almost as many people leaned toward the loyalists' camp, siding with the British. The other half were more or less apathetic. They were simply not engaged in the cause and were content to remain on the sidelines, waiting to see when, and which way, the tide would turn.

Washington was a realist. He accepted the charge of commander in chief, fully aware of its responsibilities and with his eyes wide open. And once Washington accepted a task, there was no turning back. Washington did occasionally complain about his troubles to family and friends, but publicly he was willing to accept burden after burden with good grace and a noble stoicism. His long-term vision of a free nation always remained at the forefront of his mind.

His back was strong.

Shouldering the Blame   When the Virginia Assembly criticized the actions of Washington's regiment following the loss of Fort Necessity in 1754, he responded, "I find that my own character must of necessity be involved in the general censure, for which reason I cannot help observing that if the country think they have cause to condemn my conduct and have a person in view that will act, then he may do so."[1]

Washington accepted personal responsibility for the failure and admitted that it was a weakness in his own character that allowed such a loss to take place. And he followed through on his full acknowledgment of personal responsibility by accepting condemnation from his country. Very little criticism materialized, partly because Washington was so self-effacing. He fell on his sword with dignity and finesse, and as a result, the people remembered his honesty and bravery more than his mistakes.

He Couldn't Say No   As he was about to take command of the Continental Army, Washington wrote to his beloved wife,

"[I]t was utterly out of my power to refuse this appointment, without exposing my character to such censures as would have reflected dishonor upon myself, and given pain to my friends."[2] He plainly and unequivocally believed the acceptance of responsibility to be an essential aspect of character, and refusing responsibility to be an act of dishonor.

Honor and Humanity   As discussed in Leadership Lesson #2, "A Leader Is Honest," Washington was a stickler for acting with integrity—and insisting that those in his charge do likewise.

One factor that helped turn the tide toward the cause of the revolutionaries was the British soldiers' mistreatment of landowners and everyday citizens, particularly in the south. While the redcoats plundered nearby farms, Washington did a far better job of maintaining order and respect among his soldiers. In November 1778, he wrote to Major General Israel Putnam, "You are to take every measure to prevent and severely punish marauding or any insults to the persons or destruction of the property of the inhabitants by the Soldiery."[3]

He demanded that the army take care of its own needs, so that neighbors would not become resentful. He extrapolated, on a grand scale, his own sense of personal responsibility, and demanded it of his men.

A month later, in General Orders issued on his behalf by William Alexander, Lord Stirling from headquarters, Washington felt compelled ". . . to urge officers of all ranks to search out and bring to severe and immediate punishment every soldier who shall presume to burn or otherwise destroy rails, or any part of the Farmers' enclosures. Honor and Humanity dictate that we should carefully preserve the property of our fellow Citizens."[4]

Soldiers with Character   To support his vision of a free America, Washington also maintained a vision of a loyal, efficient, and strong army. And he felt that what the army lacked in training and experience would be offset by determination and character. Not everyone followed his lead, however. Fairly early in the Revolutionary War, one of Washington's military bodyguards was involved in a plot to kidnap or kill the commander in chief. His name was Thomas Hickey, and he was captured, court-martialed, and sentenced to death by hanging. On June 28, 1776, General Washington, as leader of the Continental Army, made an entry in his orderly book that spoke to his vision of an army manned by soldiers with character: "The unhappy Fate of Thomas Hickey, executed this day for Mutiny, Sedition, and Treachery, the General hopes will be a warning to every soldier, in the Army, to avoid those crimes and all others, so disgraceful to the character of a soldier and pernicious to his country, whose pay he receives and bread he eats."[5] In essence, Washington is saying that it is not enough for just the army's leaders to have character—each and every soldier is expected to represent his nation in a respectable manner.

In a similar fashion, corporations that set high standards in terms of not just performance, but values, are creating a culture that brings out the best in people.

Admiral Garry R. White of the U.S. Navy practiced what he preached when he served as the commanding officer of the *U.S.S. George Washington,* which he described as "a completely self-contained city" with some 5,000 residents (sailors), who averaged a remarkably young 20 years old. When the ship was at sea, Captain White himself was the judge and jury for sailors who went astray. His approach was straightforward: We all make mistakes, but it's how we atone for them that makes all the difference in the world. Sailors who admitted their wrongdoings and were genuinely remorseful for their crimes were generally given a second chance. Captain White was looking for integrity—not perfection. But those who made excuses or treated their mistakes in a casual fashion were given the harshest punishment. And unless this attitude changed quickly and dramatically, the sailor was usually discharged from the navy.

The sailors themselves adopted the official logo for the ship—"The Spirit of Freedom"—a phrase George Washington used in a letter to a fellow patriot. General Washington and Captain White understood that a true spirit cannot exist unless every member of the team adopts a sense of personal responsibility for the character and reputation of the team as a whole.

As If They Were His Own   Although personally childless, Washington accepted the responsibilities of being a (step)parent and grandparent, and also supported the education of several nephews and other relatives. And this magnanimity was not superficial or half-hearted. He really cared. Even though Washington was forced to be an absentee parent for much of his life, his family was clearly important to him. Home really was where his heart remained, and as he once wrote to David Stuart, "I can truly say I had rather be at Mount Vernon with a friend or two about me, than to be attended at the Seat of Government by the Officers of State and the Representatives of every Power in Europe."[6]

All for the Cause   When Washington accepted the position of commander in chief of the Continental Army in the summer of 1775, very few others had made such a high level of personal commitment to the cause of liberty. In fact, the Declaration of Independence was not written until a year later, after Washington had achieved some encouraging success on the battlefield. The point is this: George Washington placed his life, his family, his land, and his considerable fortune on the line. He backed up his beliefs by hazarding everything he had, and he did this for all the right reasons. He knew that victory would be a tremendous uphill climb, against all odds, yet what would be his spoils? Great honor perhaps, but little else. What he truly cared about most was participating in the birth of a new republic for and by the people.

Semper Fi   Washington would have been a fan of a motto often used by the U.S. Marines: Whether it's easy or hard, whether it's good for you personally or not, do the right thing. Be "always faithful" to your cause.

Investing in the Future   Washington deserves to be spoken of in the same breath as later altruistic financiers like John D. Rockefeller, W. K. Kellogg, and Andrew Mellon, men who gave back to society much of what their families had garnered through wildly successful business ventures.

Particularly in his later years, Washington personally became an active and involved philanthropist, especially on behalf of education.

A donation to a small school in Lexington, Virginia, helped it to become the great Washington and Lee University. And about five hours away, in the port city of Chestertown, Maryland, he helped to found Washington College. By becoming chancellor of the College of William & Mary in Williamsburg (Jefferson's alma mater), Washington under-lined his desire for the brightest minds in America to remain in America for higher education—he found it distasteful that wealthy Americans were still sending their sons to England for schooling.

Closer to home, Washington was the principal benefactor of the Alexandria Academy, a school for the underprivileged that has been restored in the heart of Old Town Alexandria in Virginia.

In his will, Washington also allocated 50 shares of stock for the creation of a national university in the new nation's capital. Unfortunately, the stock was in the soon-to-be-bankrupt Potowmack Canal Company. So, alas, we must live with the fact that although several universities have been kind enough to honor George Washington in their names, there is no university that can be rightfully described as Mr. Washington's university in the same way that the University of Virginia will always be associated with Thomas Jefferson.

But in terms of their business acumen, there is no comparison between Jefferson and Washington. Jefferson died deep in debt because of his wildly extravagant expenditures. Washington, however, by almost any standards, died a wealthy man. He was justifiably proud of his assets, and he felt a special sense of self-satisfaction that his beloved Mount Vernon estate had been amassed through his own careful and prudent management. And because he carefully managed his resources, Washington had the funds necessary to free his slaves. His colleague in Charlottesville, however, was so broke that he never had this choice.

Washington passed away confident that, through his own efforts, many of his investments in the new nation had already paid off and a bright future was still to come.

Lonely at the Top   Although Washington's men thought the world of him, it would be a mistake to imagine the commander in chief as "one of the boys." By design, he maintained an appropriate distance between himself and the enlisted men, and he was by no means familiar with his officers. Washington did not want personal relationships to unduly influence the decision-making process, and he wanted to avoid the appearance of playing favorites.

Washington paid a high price to maintain his reputation

for utmost fairness. In essence, he had a challenging time making close friends. Washington had untold admirers, of course, and through letters he kept in touch with a fairly wide circle of acquaintances, but he seemed to confide in no one except his wife. Thankfully, Washington's shoulders were broad enough to accept a long list of burdens, including a certain degree of loneliness at the top.

Leadership Lesson 7

A Leader Is Determined

A leader, once convinced a particular course of action is the right one, must have the determination to stick with it and be undaunted when the going gets tough.

—RONALD REAGAN

*M*any historians feel that determination—unwavering resolve—may be George Washington's single most important character trait.

The beloved American poet James Whitcomb Riley said of achieving success, "The most essential factor is persistence—the determination never to allow your energy or enthusiasm to be dampened by the discouragement that must inevitably come."[1]

George Washington was certainly persistent. During the darkest days of the struggle for liberty, when others were more than willing to capitulate to the British, Washington battled on. He simply refused to give up. His personal determination served as a great inspiration to his soldiers during the most discouraging—and depressing—periods of the Revolutionary War.

This same tenacity was reflected in his expansive, open-minded approach to agriculture, animal husbandry, and the construction of the canal system. He was equally insistent that the presidency not become a monarchy and that he would not die before granting freedom to his slaves.

Scholars have often commented that the British did not lose the revolution on the battlefield, but rather that George Washington simply would not give up and go home. Because the Americans were so clearly outmanned and outgunned by a powerful British army (the most powerful in the world at the time), many onlookers thought it was just a matter of time before Washington surrendered. But he was determined to fight, and fight he did. He simply refused to accept defeat.

The Turning Point   Many of Washington's most trusted officers felt that crossing the Delaware River on December 25, 1776, was much too great a risk. Many of them considered it a near-suicidal mission, and, to be fair, they did have a point.

In the late summer of 1776,[2] the American army was encamped along the Pennsylvania shore of the Delaware River because, quite frankly, they had no place else to go. Washington was in the midst of a terrible losing streak during which his army had been forced off Long Island into Manhattan, forced from Manhattan into New Jersey, and forced from New Jersey into Pennsylvania. Washington knew it was just days before the expiration of the tour of duty for many of his troops, and he was well aware that the entire war was at a turning point.

So Washington asked for the advice of his most trusted officers, and then, generally speaking, he ignored their counsel. He did not put his decision up for a vote. He knew the choices were few, and he did not consider failure an option.

On Christmas Eve 1776, Washington and his troops piled into boats and set out across the Delaware in weather that was, quite possibly, the worst imaginable for a nighttime water crossing. It was snowing hard, temperatures were frigid, and the fierce winds were relentless. Adding to the misery was the fact that many of Washington's men had no shoes or boots. The river itself was treacherous. One of Washington's soldiers, Elisha Bostwick, later wrote, ". . . obstructions of ice in the river did not all get across till quite late in the evening, and all the time a constant fall of snow . . ."[3]

Washington and his troops attacked Trenton the following morning, and the Hessians quickly surrendered. Throughout the battle, Washington moved among his men, encouraging and reassuring them. Bostwick recalled hearing the general saying, "Soldiers, keep by your officers. For God's sake, keep by your officers!"[4]

Not only did Washington's victory prove to be a turning point in the war, it also persuaded many of his men—weary, worn-out men who held in their hearts dreams of heading home—to renew their enlistments. Washington's personal determination not to be defeated literally turned the tide of the war and made possible the seemingly impossible. His entreaty to his men, probably inspired by Shakespeare's "band of brothers" speech in *Henry V* (as noted by David McCullough in his 2005 speech at Brigham Young University[5]) still resonates as a clarion call for the "cause of liberty":

> My brave fellows, you have done all I asked you to do, and more than could be reasonably expected, but your country is at stake, your wives, your houses, and all that you hold dear. You have worn yourselves out with fatigues and hardships, but we know not how to spare you. If you will consent to stay one month longer, you will render that service to the cause of

liberty, and to your country, which you can probably never do under any other circumstance.[6]

Never Surrender   No matter what the odds, and no matter how dire things looked, Washington never considered a traditional surrender of his Continental Army as an option in the Revolutionary War. Why? Because the consequences would be unacceptable: death, something Washington never particularly feared, and disgrace, which is what Washington feared the most.

Yet Washington always understood that defeat was a real possibility. He never publicly acknowledged it, but privately it was obvious he had thought about it. After all, he was a realist. Exemplary of his character and commitment, though, his perception of defeat did not apply to him *personally.* In 1776, Washington wrote to his friend Burwell Bassett that his western lands on the Ohio River might prove to be an escape option if the entire revolution fell apart. He noted, ". . . in the worst event they will serve for an asylum."[7]

In modern terms, one can imagine Washington and a few of his men retreating to the wilderness, where they would adopt guerrilla warfare tactics to continue to fight against the crown.

This is proof of how determined Washington actually was: He was unequivocally prepared to fight to the death.

The Peaceable Transfer of Power   Prior to the birth of America, throughout world history, transfers of governmental power had traditionally been accomplished through either bloodlines or bloodshed. Sons and daughters ascended to thrones; monarchs were overthrown. The people—the masses of the governed—had little, if anything, to say about who would have authority over them.

The creation of the American form of government—of the people, by the people, and for the people—changed all that, with its special emphasis on the "consent of the governed." That said, though, many new Americans were doubtful that the peaceful transfer of power from one generation to another would actually take place.

As has been said many times, Washington could have been America's first king. In all likelihood, he could have also determined who would have succeeded him in power.

But Washington refused to allow the presidency to mimic monarchy, and he also was determined that the transition of power in his young nation would always be orderly, systematic, and regular. He refused absolutely all those who tried to convince him to accept a third term, partly because he was fearful of dying in office. What would happen then? Washington wanted to *personally* supervise the transfer of authority, to make sure it happened in an appropriate manner. Fortunately, Washington's example is two centuries old and still going strong.

The greatest chief executives today, regardless of the type of business, recognize the importance of finding a successor and making sure the mantle of power is passed along in a seamless fashion.

Winning When It Counts, Losing When It Doesn't

Interestingly, as incredibly competitive and determined as Washington was, he did not appear to be a bad loser—which speaks vividly to his character. Washington's expensive Arabian racehorse, Magnolia, apparently lost more races than he won. Yet it took Magnolia losing a match race to a roan colt owned by Thomas Jefferson for Washington to retire from the horse-racing arena. He ultimately traded Magnolia for 5,000 acres of land in Kentucky.[8] (Washington was also, let us not forget, a pragmatist.)

It appears that Washington also gambled at cards, and there are no mentions in his diaries that he ever came up the big winner—nor that he was particularly dismayed by his losses.

Washington knew how to keep things in perspective. He was most determined and most competitive when the stakes were highest.

How does this translate into modern terms? Many corporate executives love to compete in golf or handball as much as they do in business, but the best ones understand the difference. One is a sport, the other an important aspect of many people's lives beyond their own. The stakes really do make a difference.

The Hunt Must Go On   Washington was an extraordinarily determined foxhunter. He was often the first to start and the last to finish many hunts, and his diaries record time and time again that he was on the trail for five to seven hours, sometimes to no avail. On many occasions, the other hunters had long since fallen by the wayside. On March 2, 1768, Washington noted in his diary that he was "Hunting again, & catchd a fox with a bobd Tail & cut Ears, after 7 hours chase in wch. most of the Dogs were worsted." The following days' entries, however, reveal that Washington was most likely ill while on the hunt. He wrote on March 3, "Returnd home much disorderd by a Lax, Griping and violent straining," and on the fourth, "At Home, worse with the above complaints. Sent for Doctr. Rumney, who came in the Afternn."[9] He had worn out not only the dogs, but perhaps himself as well. Washington had insisted on continuing the hunt regardless of his poor health, perhaps because of his commitment to his other guests. Or did he simply find the chase irresistible?

Leadership Lesson 8

~

A Leader Has a Strong Work Ethic

Work is not a curse, it is the prerogative of intelligence, the only means to manhood and the measure of civilization.
—CALVIN COOLIDGE

What work I have done I have done because it has been play. If it had been work I shouldn't have done it. Who was it who said, "Blessed is the man who has found his work"? Whoever it was he had the right idea in his mind. Mark you, he says his work—not somebody else's work. The work that is really a man's own work is play and not work at all.
—MARK TWAIN

[W]hen Men are employ'd they are best contented.
—BENJAMIN FRANKLIN

A work ethic "is a set of values based on the moral virtues of hard work and diligence. It is also a belief in [the] moral benefit of work and its ability to enhance character."[1]

Washington was not born into wealth (although it can be said his family was comfortable), and we know that he was not a gentried child whose every need was seen to by a coterie of servants and slaves. Not being raised with the proverbial silver spoon in his mouth, however, inculcated in Washington from the beginning an awareness that success would require hard work and determination.

He once wrote to a nephew, "Time is limited, every hour misspent is lost forever."[2] From a very young age, Washington had watched friends and family die around him far too early, so he embraced the mature (and realistic) outlook that life was fragile. And brief. He valued time as a priceless commodity, and he tried to cram an incredible amount of work—and occasionally a little play—into every single day.

It should be noted that throughout his life Washington's energy level was consistently high, and that he was a "workaholic" in the most positive sense: He always had new projects and plans on the horizon. His strong work ethic complemented his visionary outlook.

And speaking of play, it is indicative of the man that even when Washington indulged in what he would probably describe as "idle time," he often spent it reading books on agriculture, farming, religion, politics, and government. Even his "leisure" pursuits were purposeful and instructive.

An Early Start   Washington started his own surveying business when he was 17 years old, and his fairness, diligence, and eagerness resulted in the business becoming an immediate success. With his earnings, Washington was able to purchase land, thus beginning the process of building wealth through the acquisition of property, one principal path to prominence in eighteenth-century Virginia.

Even today, it is surprising how many successful executives got early starts in the business world, often in high school and college.

Early to Rise   Washington envisioned Mount Vernon as a bustling, productive plantation that would serve as an example to his neighbors of what could result from proper land management, crop production, and marketing savvy.

His "workers" (which is how he sometimes referred to his slaves) did not always share this ethic, however.

Still, he never gave up trying to inspire all those around him. His approach toward the amount of work that needed to be done at Mount Vernon—and it was vast—was leadership by example. Even at the age of 65, Washington was up early and working hard, and he expected his slaves to do likewise. In a letter to his friend James McHenry, Washington wrote, "I begin my diurnal course with the sun, and if my hirelings are not in their places at that time I send them messages of sorrow for their indisposition."[3]

"Busy" Doesn't Even Come Close   George Washington's daily routine would exhaust the most ambitious and robust of men. He awoke between four and five in the morning, immediately dressed, left the house, and then generally rode several miles on horseback to check on work at his farms, which covered a span of 8,000 acres. A few hours later, at seven o'clock, he would return to the Mansion and join (the inevitable and unavoidable) guests for breakfast.

Because Mount Vernon was a haven for family, friends, and strangers alike—we know the Washingtons entertained hundreds of overnight guests in a single year—Washington was forced to be a reasonably polite host until well into the evening.

Meanwhile, he was an avid reader and a remarkably prolific writer—his papers, currently being assembled by *The Papers of George Washington* project at the University of Virginia, will eventually fill more than 90 separate volumes.

He is thought to have written more than 20,000 individual letters! Where *did* he find the time?

A Deeper Understanding   Washington was often frustrated that others in his family and circle of influence did not work nearly as hard as they should. His stepson Jacky (John Parke Custis, Martha's third child with Daniel Parke Custis) was a bit of a problem child who never applied himself at school. This was especially frustrating to the general, but he usually gave in to the wishes of his wife, who was an easy touch. Also, some of Washington's slaves were especially creative in coming up with ways to avoid work.

But this came as no surprise to Washington—he was an insightful man. He could see beyond the quotidian and had the capability of a deeper understanding of the "whys" of a situation—always the mark of an effective leader. Washington, as a true believer in the free market system, realized that one of the weaknesses of the institution of slavery was the lack of incentives. Why should a slave work hard? Aside from fear of punishment, were there any real rewards a hardworking slave could reap? Washington actually tried to introduce some incentives—better clothing, a more desirable job, even a little cold, hard cash. But they just weren't enough to inspire the quantity and quality of work Washington desired.

Washington knew that the American economy would be strongest and most effective as a free market–based system that rewarded effort and hard work—a true meritocracy, functioning effectively regardless of an individual's social class. His experience dealing with his slaves starkly illustrated for him the reality of this type of system: A strong work ethic is ultimately meaningless if a worker's effort is not rewarded. Aside from Washington's moral aversion to the institution of slavery, he was also able to see beyond the humanistic factor and look at it as an object lesson. As we have seen over and over, Washington was a pragmatist. And his deeper understanding of the distorted economy of the slavery system not only convinced him that slavery could not survive in the new country, but also supported his deeply held belief in a free market as the engine of progress and growth. As Washington said in an October 10, 1784, letter to Benjamin Harrison, "A people . . . who are possessed of the spirit of commerce, who see, and who will pursue their advantages, may achieve almost anything."[4]

An Eye for Opportunity   While in his 30s, Washington loaned $3,750 to one of his neighbors, Captain John Posey, who owned a ferry service across the Potomac. When Posey defaulted on the loan, Washington acquired the business and, rather than sell it, operated it himself from 1769 to 1790. He continued the service for a year and a half after becoming president. Passengers crossing the river in 1789 and 1790 may not have known that they were riding the president's ferry!

At the Front   In the eight years of the Revolutionary War, George Washington never took a vacation, evincing a personal commitment to his work that was simply unheard of at the time (and which remains incredibly rare today). He maintained a single-minded focus on the cause of liberty, the welfare of his men, and the future of his nascent country.

Mrs. Washington visited his encampments with great frequency—she traveled to him every winter for the duration of the war. Despite the difficulty of travel, she took the initiative because she knew he would never leave the troops to visit her. Her commitment to her husband and his mission was complete, and when the days are totaled, she was with him for about half of the period of the war. In an age when officers were almost always well-heeled noblemen—and acted like it—Washington broke the mold and remained at the side of his men. She, in turn, was at his side as much as possible.

Washington did not sit in a comfortable office many miles behind the lines—he led from the front. A diligent—and apparently tireless—leader like Washington did not ask his men to do anything he personally would not do, and this included working ceaselessly at their common endeavor.

Working for the Good   Washington never looked at the presidency as an honorary position—it was instead an extremely demanding job. When Congress approved a then staggeringly high compensation of $25,000 (over $500,000 in today's funds), Washington declined the salary and simply asked for his out-of-pocket expenses to be covered. He believed in working diligently for the common cause rather than personal gain. His noble motives notwithstanding, Congress decided not to take him up on his offer. They insisted that he accept the salary. In turn, he spent close to $2,000 of his salary on presidential entertaining.[5]

Against Doctor's Orders   To Washington, his efforts on behalf of his nation took precedence, even over his health. In a letter to Lafayette, he talks about putting his work first: "I have, a few days since, had a severe attack of the peripneumony kind: but am now recovered, except in point of strength. My Physicians advise me to more exercise and less application to business. I cannot, however, avoid persuading myself, that it is essential to accomplish whatever I have undertaken . . . to the best of my abilities."[6]

Leadership Lesson 9

❧

A Leader Uses Good Judgment

One cool judgment is worth a thousand hasty counsels. The thing to be supplied is light, not heat.

—WOODROW WILSON

Perhaps the strongest feature in [Washington's] character was prudence, never acting until every circumstance, every consideration, was maturely weighed; refraining if he saw a doubt, but, when once decided, going through with his purpose, whatever obstacles opposed.

—THOMAS JEFFERSON[1]

*W*hat is good judgment? It is, in its purest and most potent form, the ability to make smart decisions. Those possessing this talent—like George Washington—are capable of processing a myriad of information pertaining to a particular situation and quickly determining the best course of action.

Washington was the ultimate decision maker, and, as president, he was well aware that a great burden rested on his shoulders. The buck really did stop on George Washington's desk, again and again. The people of America trusted George

Washington more than any other Founding Father—trust and confidence, remember?—largely because he made the correct decisions, and usually for all the right reasons.

It is important to note, too, that Washington did not take opinion polls and make decisions based on what would be the most popular course of action—which, as we know, is an all-too-common political practice today. He sometimes went against the advice of his colleagues, and he occasionally took a stand that was far from popular. Yet his judgment was keen, and once he had made his decision, his commitment to a course of action was steadfast.

Looking back with the luxury of hindsight, we now know that Washington's track record in terms of making correct decisions remains virtually unbeatable. And to the credit of our earliest American citizens, the majority of the people seemed to recognize and appreciate this.

The General's Good Judgment   On July 31, 1777, the Second Continental Congress appointed the 19-year-old French Marquis de Lafayette a major general in the Continental Army.

Washington's officers were less than pleased about this development; in fact, many were outraged that a very young French nobleman (the word "teenager" had not yet been coined) would have the audacity to expect an appointment as a full-fledged general.

But Washington knew that his fledgling nation would not achieve victory over the British without support from the French. Plus, Washington liked what he saw in Lafayette, who, albeit young, was closely connected to the right people in France. He also brought with him tremendous energy and enthusiasm—he truly believed in the American cause.

Washington and Lafayette, men representing very different backgrounds, ultimately became the best of friends. They developed a warm father-son type of relationship, and together spearheaded a partnership between two nations that did indeed result in the defeat of the British. This could happen only because George Washington kept an open mind. He must have been skeptical that a 19-year-old foreigner would be an effective leader in an American war, but he gave the kid a chance—just as Washington himself had been given a breakthrough opportunity 20 years earlier in the French and Indian War.

The Bookseller and the Quaker Washington was a strong judge of character, and he often valued loyalty and integrity more than quantifiable experience.

In 1775, Nathanael Greene, a foundryman, politician, militiaman, and Quaker, pulled together a band of soldiers to assist the American army around Boston. Greene had a pronounced limp, however, and his military knowledge and experience were not enough to overcome first impressions. To many onlookers, Greene's physical disability rendered him incapable of serving as an officer. In fact, Congress refused to grant him an officer's commission. But Greene was so committed to the cause that he willingly served as a private. His devotion to independence and his extraordinary military mind gradually became obvious, and in March 1776, Washington ordered Greene to take command of the city of Boston.

Henry Knox was a bookseller who volunteered to serve in the Continental Army and fought at the Battle of Bunker Hill. Although self-taught and possessing little military experience, Knox impressed Washington immediately. Knox's voluminous reading had provided him with wide-ranging military knowledge, and his exemplary service during the Revolutionary War resulted in his appointment by Washington as the nation's first secretary of war. He was a critical mover and shaker in the creation of the U.S. Navy.

Washington intuitively recognized the quality and potential of both Greene and Knox. Renowned historian David McCullough, in a 2005 speech at Brigham Young University, said of the two men, "Nathanael Greene and Henry Knox, along with Washington, were to be the only general officers in the Revolutionary War who stayed until the very end. So Washington's judgment could not have been better. Nathanael Greene turned out to be the best general we had, and I'm including Washington in that lineup—Greene, the Quaker with a limp, the man who knew nothing but what he had read in books, who, like Washington, learned from his mistakes."[2]

Selecting strong subordinates is never as easy as it looks. When he was 30 years old, General Electric's longtime CEO, Jack Welch, remembers that he factored in a candidate's appearance far more than he should have. After all, doesn't a vice president of public relations have to look good? He also felt most comfortable selecting Japanese executives who spoke easy-to-understand English. But it did not take long for him to realize that neither looks nor language were the key talents he was really looking for.[3]

In most cases, Washington demonstrated a knack for cutting through the superficial aspects of a potential leader and getting to his core. That's how a Quaker with a limp and a bookseller who tipped the scales at 300 pounds could climb to the top of the ladder.

The First Team of Rivals   The idea of forming a cabinet of presidential policy advisors and government department heads was Washington's own. No such body was defined by the Constitution. And when considering who specifically he, as president, would bring into his inner circle, Washington selected men not based on their politics, but on their talents.

When Jack Welch set about transforming GE, he took a

similar approach. "Change doesn't come from a slogan or a speech. It happens because you put the right people in place to make it happen. People first. Strategy and everything else second."[4]

That's why Washington's cabinet was so successful, and why the concept of a cabinet has survived ever since. Thomas Jefferson (secretary of state), Alexander Hamilton (secretary of the treasury), Henry Knox (secretary of war), and Edmund Randolph (attorney general) were all men Washington knew well, trusted, and admired (although the trust factor did indeed deteriorate before Washington's presidency came to a close).

Washington liked the fact that Hamilton and Jefferson usually held opposing views—he knew that both were certainly worth listening to, at the very least. Washington also realized that conflict is a natural and necessary component of progress. It did him—and the country—no good to have weak yes-men as his advisors.

In creating a more modern list of leadership tenets, General Julius Becton of the U.S. Army noted, "Disagreement is not disrespect." Washington encouraged his subordinates to express their opinions, for better or worse.

Ultimately, though, Washington accepted that he was the one who had to decide which direction was best for the nation. He opted to support Federalism, which advocated a strong centralized government. With this type of organization, the states deferred specific powers and rights (defense, foreign affairs, etc.) to a central government, a body which Washington and most of his cabinet members (Jefferson excluded) agreed should be strong and well-financed. For instance, as part of the Federalist ideology, Washington backed most of Hamilton's ideas to form a national bank, as well as Knox's initiative for a navy.

The bottom line is that Washington made a decision to

embrace Federalism and then stuck by it, even though he hated the concept of political parties. His judgment was again sterling, and the nation began to prosper far faster than most imagined it would.

Doris Kearns Goodwin, in her book on the political genius of Abraham Lincoln, points out that Lincoln asked his rivals for the presidency to join his cabinet—a move that shocked the nation.[5] But he wanted the most talented people, not the easiest to get along with. Actually, Lincoln was simply following in George Washington's footsteps.

The Whiskey Rebellion . . . Quashed   In 1791, as a means for paying off the enormous debts of the Revolutionary War (all of which, of course, had been assumed by the federal government, resulting in the first national debt), Congress passed an excise tax on all spirits distilled in America.

This was not a popular decision, nor was it a popular tax (if such a thing exists), especially among farmers on the western frontier who routinely distilled their crops into spirits so as not to have to transport huge amounts of grain over hundreds of miles. The spirits became for them, in a sense, currency, and they knew that the new excise tax would have a significant impact on many of their incomes.

From its initial passage, almost everyone affected by the tax expressed outrage. Citizens (most of whom imbibed, of course), local politicians, and especially farmers all spoke out against the tax. It wasn't long before the protests became physical—and violent. Tax inspectors were tarred and feathered; the local distillers who acquiesced to the tax were shunned by their neighbors.

The rebellion peaked on July 16, 1794, when 500 men attacked the home of the local excise inspector, General John Neville, in Allegheny County, Pennsylvania. Neville fought back briefly, killing two and wounding six, but he was outnumbered and ultimately fled the house. The insurgents raided and looted Neville's home, and then burned it down.

When news of the uprising reached President Washington, he was furious. In essence, he put his boot down. Hard. He knew that this was a pivotal moment in establishing the authority of the federal government. What good were federal laws if they could be ignored? Washington's subordinates recommended a studied reaction, but Washington's judgment was wide-ranging in perspective—he was, after all, a global thinker—and he quickly decided that his response needed to be strong.

On August 11, 1794, Washington issued a proclamation that was unmistakable in its message:

> [I]t is in my judgment necessary under the circumstances of the case to take measures for calling forth the militia in order to suppress the combinations aforesaid, and to cause the laws to be duly executed; and I have accordingly determined so to do, feeling the deepest regret for the occasion, but withal the most solemn conviction that the essential interests of the Union demand it, that the very existence of government and the fundamental principles of social order are materially involved in the issue, and that the patriotism and firmness of all good citizens are seriously called upon, as occasions may require, to aid in the effectual suppression of so fatal a spirit.[6]

Washington immediately ordered the formation of an enormous army. He called up a contingent of 12,950 men—more soldiers than he had commanded during many periods of the Revolutionary War—and set out for Pittsburgh. The president led the troops.

Yes, Washington felt it was incredibly important that he

himself assume command. On September 25, 1794, the massive force arrived at the site of the rebellion. But there was no fighting when the troops reached Pittsburgh. The distillers immediately backed down, as Washington almost certainly expected they would.

Washington had made his point, and it was clear to all: Federal laws were not flexible, and lawbreakers would be dealt with swiftly and decisively.

A man of action with impeccable judgment is hard to stop—particularly if that man is as powerful and respected as George Washington.

The epilogue to this story is equally interesting and important. Washington was practical enough to pardon the rebels, who were an essential part of America's burgeoning economy. So although the law was not flexible, the president's punishment was—and in this case, he used it sparingly.

The Good of the Country Comes First   During Washington's presidency, an overwhelming majority of Americans wanted the new nation to support the French wholeheartedly in their war against the British.

Jefferson (and many other respected leaders) felt it was our duty to do so, and he tried every means—some bordering on deceitful—to win over public support.

But Washington knew that his most critical job was to keep the nation together and provide an environment in which the private sector would thrive without the cost and distraction of war. So he went against public opinion and insisted upon neutrality.

He asked John Jay to negotiate a treaty with the British to avoid another armed conflict. Unfortunately, the terms Jay obtained were far from attractive to most American leaders, even those who generally supported the administration.

By signing the treaty, Washington put his personal pride aside and placed the good of his country over his own popularity. He took his hits from opposition newspapers and remained unswayed by public outcries in favor of the French.

In hindsight, Washington's judgment was not just correct—it was vital. America went from weak to strong in a few short years, and Washington's carefully thought out policy of deliberate neutrality was essential to this progress.

Leadership Lesson 10

~

A Leader Learns from Mistakes

Experience is simply the name we give our mistakes.

—OSCAR WILDE

Errors once discovered are more than half amended.

—GEORGE WASHINGTON[1]

Success is the ability to go from one failure to another with no loss of enthusiasm.

—WINSTON CHURCHILL

*I*n a July 2005 interview with *Voice of America News,* David McCullough noted that the early years of the Revolutionary War were incredibly depressing. "We lost every time we confronted the British, and very often it was Washington's fault. He had a lot to learn, but he always learned from his mistakes."[2]

In his September 2005 speech at Brigham Young University, McCullough reiterated his assessment, noting that "[Washington] made dreadful mistakes, particularly in the year 1776. They were almost inexcusable, inexplicable mistakes, but he always learned from them. And he never forgot what the fight was about—'the glorious cause of America,' as they called it. Washington would not give up; he would not quit."[3]

Washington was a lifelong learner—and his learning extended far beyond the academic. He certainly read widely to expand his knowledge of agriculture, the arts, philosophy, and the sciences, but he also embraced *real-world learning,* the kind of education that comes from making a blunder, recognizing it, and then figuring out what went wrong and how to prevent it from happening again.

Early in life, Washington was frequently arrogant and short-tempered, but the negative reactions to this behavior quickly convinced him that he needed to refine and control his temperament. Washington made numerous military errors, but he learned from them and used these experiences to set an example for others. He made political blunders, but these helped him to recognize how important it was to strengthen his relationship with Congress and to hone his diplomatic skills.

Washington was self-aware enough to admit to himself and to others that he made mistakes. He would then correct the situation if possible and move on without delay or excuses.

This is also one of the reasons he was such a successful businessman. Mac Griswold, author of a wonderful book on George Washington's horticultural activities, points out that Washington once planted something like 200 seeds sent to him from China—and not a single one came up![4] But Washington considered this a learning experience—he always came away from such failings with new knowledge, and seldom felt he had wasted his time.

A Yearning for Learning   George Washington always felt that his formal education was incomplete and deficient— which it was. He carried around an inferiority complex, because the educational achievements of his colleagues and peers were so much greater—at least on paper—than his own. Yet we know that as a young man he intuitively sought to correct this deficit by using mentors—particularly his older half-brother Lawrence and his neighbor Lord Fairfax—to learn about the ways of the world. He was also an avid reader and turned to books to supplement and expand what he considered to be his woefully inadequate formal education.

Washington is a superb example of a leader with a balanced education. He graduated summa cum laude from the school of hard knocks, but he equally appreciated how great literature and a knowledge of history can inform a leader's decisions.

Survival First   The French and Indian War provided first-hand knowledge that informed Washington's efforts in the Revolutionary War, when he would shoulder far more responsibility.

In the French and Indian War, both sides concentrated on building forts. Forts translated into controlling territory. But Washington eventually discovered that commanding forts did not necessarily translate into victory. Perhaps this fact was indelibly etched into his mind after he was forced to surrender to the French after an embarrassing defeat at Fort Necessity.

In the Revolutionary War, the British held sway over huge portions of the colonies, including our largest cities. But the Brits knew that victory was possible only if they could destroy Washington's army, either by decimating the army in battle or by taking large numbers of soldiers as prisoners.

So Washington, as loath as he was to admit it, realized that simple survival was of the utmost importance—it had to take priority as the rule of the day, every day—and he accepted that fact. He figured out how to retreat with honor, how to confuse the enemy, and how to use intelligence to outthink the British, knowing it might not be possible to outfight them.

Retreating was against the grain for an aggressive leader like Washington, but over time he learned to control his feelings and think strategically. He learned to sneak away under the cover of darkness, resolving to fight another day.

The Courage to Make Mistakes   In his self-effacing book *Jack: Straight from the Gut,* Jack Welch, the longtime CEO of GE, notes, "I've learned that mistakes can often be as good a teacher as success."[5] Like Washington, Welch admits to "stumbling" a number of times in his career, and sometimes his miscalculations cost him—and his company—quite dearly. But it never stopped him from moving forward—in fact, if anything, mistakes only made him quicken the pace.

The same can be said of Washington. Even though he usually admitted his mistakes, he didn't dwell on them—the best defense was a fresh, new offense.

Throughout his life, Washington never gave the impression that he was fearful of being fired because of these mistakes. He was always concerned that he would soil his reputation, but his decisions were not impaired by a desire to please his peers—instead, they were based on what was right for his country. Even during the darkest days of the Revolutionary War, when fellow officers were scheming with congressmen to replace the commander in chief, Washington kept his eye on the prize.

Once, when I was in my late 30s, I was told by a retired CEO that visionary leaders must take chances in order to cause change, to move an organization forward. In doing so, they willingly accept a far higher risk of being fired.

When interviewing candidates for important jobs at Mount Vernon, our current chairman, Gay Hart Gaines, always surprises people when she asks, "Have you ever been fired?" Those who quickly respond, "Of course not" (and most do), are probably taken aback by her follow-up. "My father was fired, my husband was fired, and they were both better for it." (In fact, they both became chairmen of very profitable companies.) It is surprising how many of the most successful leaders in America have been fired, or at least passed over for promotion, at least once. The fear of being fired can be stifling and counterproductive.

Not a Man Living   In recent years, a number of scholars have declared that slavery was George Washington's Achilles' heel—his fatal flaw, his ultimate failing of character. Today it is easy to say that we wish that George Washington had never owned slaves. But he did.

When he was quite young and still more a follower than a leader, Washington clearly bought into the system of slavery. In fact, he inherited his first slave when he was just 11 years old.

But what is more relevant to us today is that Washington listened to others and genuinely experienced a change of heart. The essential truth—and the truth that speaks most powerfully to our understanding of his character—is that Washington's attitude toward slavery changed dramatically during his lifetime.

During the Revolutionary War, Washington witnessed the bravery of the slaves who took our side against the king. He listened carefully to his most trusted comrades (including Lafayette), and it was not lost on him that there were numerous abolitionists, who made convincing arguments, among them. He expressed a great deal of admiration for northern farmers, many of whom were very successful without using slaves to work their farms. He asked himself, *If they can do it, why can't we?*

And most importantly, toward the end of his life, Washington came to understand that the tenets upon which our new nation were based simply could not coexist with slavery. He once wrote, "There is not a man living who wishes more sincerely than I do, to see a plan adopted for the abolition of [slavery] . . ."[6]

I truly believe Washington would have tried to eliminate the institution of slavery when he was president if he had felt that he could have done so without tearing apart the nation. But in those early years, the bonds between our states were exceedingly tenuous. The Union was hanging by a thread, and, in my opinion, that thread was George Washington. Simply put, Washington did what he thought was best for the nation.

When he retired from the presidency, Washington returned to Mount Vernon with the hope of renting much of his land to tenant farmers who would, in turn, hire the Mount Vernon slaves he hoped to free. Alas, no one answered his ads, so this plan never got off the ground. Washington did indeed free his slaves in his will, and he was the only Founding Father who did so. Thomas Jefferson lived 26 years longer, and he still failed to follow Washington's example.

Yes, owning slaves was a wrong that nothing can really ever right. But we should not allow this fact—as grievous as it might appear to us today—to overshadow what Washington accomplished and what he sacrificed to create the most free and admired nation in the entire world. Even today, total freedom for one and all is still many steps away— the struggle is a continuous one. But no single step toward freedom has taken us further than the step taken by the Founding Fathers. They established a sturdy foundation for a system of government so new and so different that the entire world took notice, and this is the foundation upon which we continue to build, working toward the promise of justice for all.

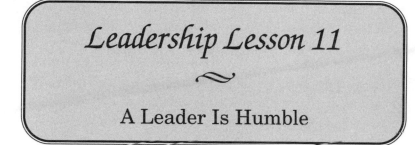

Leadership Lesson 11

A Leader Is Humble

Avoid putting yourself before others and you can become a leader among men.

—LAO-TZU

Humility must always be the portion of any man who receives acclaim earned in the blood of his followers and the sacrifices of his friends.

—DWIGHT D. EISENHOWER

I often say of George Washington that he was one of the few in the whole history of the world who was not carried away by power.

—ROBERT FROST

A leader who is a braggart is immediately suspect.
With every pat on his or her own back, motivations are puzzled over, and the leap to unfortunate conclusions can be speedy—has the leader placed his own interests and advancement over those of the ones he has been entrusted to lead?

One of the most admirable aspects of Washington's character was his sense of humility, his self-effacement, his respectful deference to others. He was quick to decline credit and quicker to assign credit to others. He was often vocal about his personally perceived shortcomings and genuinely modest when receiving praise for efforts that even he had to acknowledge (often reluctantly) were meritorious.

In today's celebrity-driven society, is anyone ever given credit for dignified modesty? It is a trait that hardly matters anymore; in fact, the antithesis of humility and modesty—that is, "blowing your own horn"—is considered in today's world proactive and ambitious.

Yet humility certainly mattered in the eighteenth century. George Washington was elected president twice with almost universal support, yet he *never campaigned for the office.* His colleagues and peers knew he was simply too modest to do so.

Washington truly believed that if a leader selflessly gave everything he had to his country, the people would recognize this sacrifice and act accordingly. They would support him in his efforts without being asked. To promote oneself, or to advertise one's talents, Washington felt, would be crass and ungentlemanly.

This is not to say that Washington lacked confidence—nothing could be further from the truth. But he was seldom cocky or arrogant like so many leaders and high-profile people today.

Washington was, in a word, gracious.

Anxious Beginnings   In a letter to Martha at the start of the Revolutionary War, Washington expressed his apprehension about being given command of the Continental Army, of being entrusted with such a profound responsibility. He wrote of his ". . . consciousness of its being a trust too great for my capacity . . ."[1]

With Utmost Sincerity   At the Second Continental Congress, upon accepting the position of commander in chief, Washington was blunt about his feelings of inadequacy: "But, lest some unlucky event should happen," he said to the gathered delegates, "unfavourable to my reputation, I beg it may be remembered, by every Gentleman in the room, that I, this day, declare with the utmost sincerity, I do not think myself equal to the Command I am honored with."[2]

Stormy Days of Life   When Washington was elected president, he wrote to Alexander Hamilton that he was accepting it "with more diffidence and reluctance than I ever experienced before in my life. It would be, however, with a fixed and sole determination of lending whatever assistance might be in my power to promote the public weal, in hopes that at a convenient and early period my services might be dispensed with, and that I might be permitted once more to retire, to pass an unclouded evening after the stormy day of life, in the bosom of domestic tranquility."[3]

Indispensable   Washington's effectiveness as a leader came in part from his commitment to the principle that he was "dispensable." This modest approach to leadership made the public trust Washington even more, which made our first president far more powerful and indispensable than any other Founding Father.

Fallible and Inferior?   In his farewell address, Washington, when speaking about his acceptance of the presidency, said, "In the discharge of this trust I will only say that I have, with good intentions, contributed toward the organization and administration of the Government the best exertions of which *a very fallible judgment* was capable." He also admitted that he knew he was "Not unconscious in the outset of *the inferiority of my qualifications* . . ."[4]

For the Right Reason   Washington's intentions were pure. In a letter to the English historian Catherine Macaulay Graham, he wrote, "All see, and most admire, the glare which hovers round the external trappings of elevated office. To me there is nothing in it, beyond the lustre which may be reflected from its connection with a power of promoting human felicity."[5]

First to Arrive   Reportedly, Washington was so embarrassed at being introduced with such pomp and circumstance at his first inaugural ball as the "President of the United States" that he subsequently arrived early. He slipped in— usually alone—so that he would not have to make a grand entrance when appearing at such an event.

Divine Munificence   Whenever Washington achieved something truly special, or whenever circumstances conspired to resolve in favor of America, he almost always gave credit to God. In doing so, he downplayed his own contributions and enabled the spotlight to shine on the many, not the few. With his typical graciousness, Washington was able to defer the praise that his country and, in fact, the world was more than ready to shower upon him.

One of Them   Washington's appearance at a small meeting-house in Newburgh, New York, was not only one of the most critical moments of his life, but one of the most critical in the life of the revolutionary cause. It was March 1783, and many of Washington's officers were fed up. Against all odds, they had successfully won the war, yet Congress had failed to pay their salaries or pensions. Rumors were spreading that the army could and should overwhelm the civilian government and put Washington in charge. There was even some talk about making Washington king. Washington's effectiveness in putting a halt to this potential coup d'etat depended in large part on his genuine sense of modesty. One of Washington's aides, Colonel David Cobb, recalled that the commander in chief reached into his pocket, pulled out an address written in his own hand, and then paused to reach again into his pocket for still something else. Washington then looked up and said, "Gentlemen, you will permit me to put on my spectacles, for I have not only grown gray, but almost blind, in the service of my country."[6]

When Washington humbly admitted that he had not only turned gray, but also gone almost blind in the service of his new nation, he clearly communicated that the war had taken its toll upon him personally. At that moment he made a special connection to his men by showing them that he was intensely human. He did not order them to do the right thing, but rather inspired them to do the right thing, and for all the right reasons.

In his speech, Washington also reminded his men that he was one of them: "I have never left your side one moment. . . . I have been the constant companion and witness of your Distresses, and not among the last to feel, and acknowledge your Merits. . . . I have ever considered my own Military reputation as inseparably connected with that of the Army. As my Heart has ever expanded with joy, when I have heard its praises, and my indignation has arisen, when the mouth of detraction has been opened against it . . ." This is Washington at his best—his performance, as one officer remembered, "drew tears" from many of those present.[7]

Many historians feel that this was the greatest single moment in Washington's public life. It's at this point that Washington separates himself from all the others, where his reputation leaps to a higher plane. Unlike the revolutionary leaders of the past, such as Julius Caesar and Oliver Cromwell, or those who followed, such as Fidel Castro and

Mao, Washington does not take advantage of his all-powerful position as a successful military leader. And he does more than just refuse the crown. He also retires from the army entirely, to ensure that the power will rest with the elected civilian government, not with the military. Simply put, Washington put down his sword and picked up his plow.

Giving up power is incredibly hard for a strong and ambitious leader to do, but Washington never hesitated. To him, it was a simple decision. Hundreds of good men had died for this cause, and he would not let them down.

But the rest of the world was shocked by this selfless action. King George III purportedly said that if Washington really gives up his power and returns to his farm, he will be "the greatest man in the world."

A generation later, after facing bitter defeat and being sent into exile, a forlorn Napoleon, near death, commented, "They expected me to be another Washington." Clearly, the famous French leader was questioning if *anyone* could ever live up to the lofty standard established by George Washington.

Washington's careful use of power—and his consistent refusal to abuse power—is one of his most enduring leadership lessons.

Respecting the Office   The date is Saturday, March 4, 1797. Washington's diary entry for this day was the very definition of understatement: "Much such a day as yesterday in all respects. Mercury at 41."[8] He was, of course, commenting on the weather, yet this day was certainly quite different in at least one respect: It was the day George Washington would turn over the presidency to John Adams, the new president-elect.

As Washington had been known to do in the past when his presence had been required, he arrived early at Federal Hall in Philadelphia for Adams's inauguration. He took his seat on the dais next to Thomas Jefferson, the vice president-elect, and listened intently to Adams's inaugural address (in which Adams made special mention of outgoing President Washington's warning about avoiding foreign entanglements).

After Adams's remarks, Washington deliberately requested that Jefferson speak next. Jefferson was the younger man, and he was also accustomed to deferring to Washington simply out of respect. But Washington was having none of it. Thomas Jefferson was now the vice president and it was his proper place to speak after the president. After all, Washington was now simply a citizen of the United States, a position he accepted with great enthusiasm.

Washington also insisted that the new president and vice president go before him when they departed the building to greet the crowd. Washington stepped aside for the new chief executive with his customary grace and dignity.

This peaceful transfer of power is rightfully considered Washington's greatest gift to his nation.

Counterpoint: *The Young Washington*

The Folly of Youth

In a presentation at Columbia University called "George Washington and the Legacy of Character," historians Dorothy Twohig, Peter Henriques, and Don Higginbotham made the point that Washington's humility and sense of self-effacement evolved over time. "The young Washington," they noted, "is brash, argumentative, impatient, greedy for land and possessions, in hot pursuit of a commission in the British army, often not particularly likable, but very human."[9]

What made Washington so arrogant as a young man? This trio of scholars believed it was the early death of his father and what they describe as his "lifelong incompatibility"[10] with his mother. The vagaries of his parents and the circumstances of his early years fostered in Washington a realization that he needed to be independent, self-reliant, and what we would describe today as "proactive."

But as is often the case with the untried and the unseasoned, there was a tendency by Washington to be *too* outspoken and *too* aggressive. And his surviving letters illustrate this initial arrogance.

The fact that Washington could transform himself into a leader known for his modesty and dignity speaks to his self-control and determination, as well as his ability to learn from mistakes.

A Leader Does the Research and Development

He who does not research has nothing to teach.

—PROVERB

*G*eorge Washington was, to use an anachronistic term to describe someone from the eighteenth century, "hard-wired" to conduct research. From an early age he knew that he had to learn from hands-on experience because his formal education was quite limited. He intuitively understood the process of research and its application to real-world problems and situations.

In addition to his need for knowledge in his roles as commander in chief of the Continental Army and, later, president, Washington was also aggressive and creative in coming up with innovations in his business ventures, ways of improving his farming practices, and even new takes on architectural design.

The mature Washington was, for the most part, thoughtful and careful rather than reckless, in marked contrast to the impulsive young soldier in the French and Indian War. But this does not mean that he did not take chances and risk failure. He definitely believed in and put into practice the adage

"No guts, no glory." He seldom took shortcuts or the easiest path. His research was sometimes so thorough and meticulous that it probably drove his subordinates crazy. For instance, it is hard to imagine why Washington felt it was so important to figure out that a bushel of timothy seeds included some 13,410,000 individual kernels. But he did.

What is important to remember is that most of Washington's business ventures were not designed just to better his own bottom line. Deliberately, and consistently, Washington sought to find new ways of making America more productive because he instinctively knew that the free market system rewarded creativity and risk taking. But Washington liked to take risks only after a thorough process of research and development—he liked to "do his homework first."

We look in depth at Washington as an entrepreneur in Part III, but here is an overview of how Washington encouraged research and learning, always with an eye toward furthering the American economy. Washington was well aware that he was setting an example for others to follow.

An Early Environmentalist   Washington spent years testing new crop rotations, systematically experimenting and always keeping in mind his two primary goals, which were sometimes in conflict. He wanted to reinvigorate the soil, yet he also wanted to maximize the production of cash crops. In the long term, Washington knew that enhancing the health of the soil would result in the enrichment of his bank account.

Always an Eye for Improvements   Washington designed a new kind of barrel seeder that combined the plowing of fields and the placement of seeds into a single action. With this piece of equipment, Washington conserved both energy and time. Washington was equally aggressive in terms of his cutting-edge approach to animal husbandry, his gristmill, and his distillery. He studied, contemplated, conceived, and acted. George Washington would have felt right at home in most any research facility operating today: He understood the underlying process, and he valued results that were based on careful experimentation rather than casual observation.

Indispensably Requisite   In an age when "gentlemen farmers" often acted intuitively rather than rationally, Washington appreciated far more than most the cut-and-dried aspect of mathematics. In January 1788, mathematician Nicholas Pike sent Washington a copy of his new book, *A System of Arithmetic,* one of the first mathematics textbooks published in America. It took Washington six months to respond to Pike, but when he did he was effusive in his praise for Pike's work, obviously delighted that it was "an American production." He also acknowledged his deference to those who knew more about arithmetic than he himself did, while recognizing the contribution Pike had made to "civilised life":

> The science of figures, to a certain degree, is not only indispensably requisite in every walk of civilised life; but the investigation of mathematical truths accustoms the mind to method and correctness in reasoning, and is an employment peculiarly worthy of rational beings. In a clouded state of existence, where so many things appear precarious to the bewildered research, it is here that the rational faculties find a firm foundation to rest upon. From the high ground of mathematical and philosophical demonstration, we are insensibly led to far nobler speculations and sublimer meditations.

Washington then expressed his deep and abiding interes in the "encouragement of American Genius," concluding b telling Pike that "no one will be more highly gratified with the success of your ingenious, arduous and useful undertaking than he, who has the unfeigned pleasure to subscribe himself."[1]

Frugal to the End   Like most good businessmen, Washington refrained from becoming so involved with or enamored of a new venture that he lost his perspective, particularly in the financial sense. Few projects were closer to his heart than the construction of the new capital city and the home of the first chief executive, even though, in his heart, Washington knew that there was little chance he would remain president long enough to take up residence there. During the planning phase of the project, when the president learned that a 20 percent increase in square footage would result in a far greater increase in the construction budget, Washington made his stance clear. "I confess that I cannot see how so great an increase of expence would arise from the small encrease of dimensions proposed," noted Washington. "I am decidedly of opinion that it would be best to take the plan on it's original scale as you mention."[2] Washington knew that good CEOs do not become so emotionally attached that they ignore the strong business acumen that got them there in the first place. How many good people have been troubled by a bad construction decision, when they simply needed to say "enough is enough"?

Ease of Transport Equals Commerce   In 1784, at the conclusion of the Revolutionary War, Washington returned to Mount Vernon after more than eight years away from his beloved sanctuary. Still five years from accepting his first presidential term, Washington busied himself repairing neglected buildings and seeing to the demands of his busy estate.

In addition to his efforts at Mount Vernon, Washington also redoubled his determination to construct a canal system on the Potomac to fulfill his ultimate vision to connect the Ohio Valley (he called it the "howling wilderness"[3]) with established eastern markets.

Washington's plans for the Potomac Canal were incredibly bold, and the engineering required to make his dream a reality was probably reaching a bit too far. In general, the project was deemed a failure. But Washington died feeling that the canal venture was worth the valiant effort, and I tend to agree—it was an incredibly bold stroke inspired by Washington's grand vision for America. (See Part III for details on Washington's Potomac Canal plan.)

At the Forefront of Inoculation   During his only trip outside America, Washington came down with smallpox on the Caribbean island of Barbados. He was only 19 and, in all likelihood, the picture of health, so he was able to rebound from the disease in a matter of weeks. The resulting immunity protected him as tens of thousands of soldiers fell ill from the highly contagious sickness throughout the Revolutionary War. While many other influential leaders—including some doctors—opposed inoculation for smallpox, Washington became one of its biggest advocates. He was not afraid to implement a relatively new medical practice on a widespread basis, and many soldiers survived to fight another day because of this decision. As historian Joseph Ellis notes in his latest book, *His Excellency,* "A compelling case can be made tha [Washington's] swift response to the smallpox epidemic a to a policy of inoculation was the most important strat decision of his military career."[4]

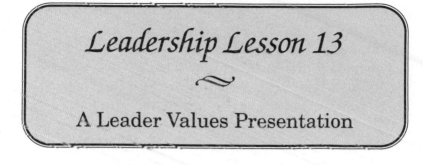

Leadership Lesson 13

A Leader Values Presentation

Our work is the presentation of our capabilities.
—JOHANN WOLFGANG VON GOETHE

*I*t seems like a contradiction, perhaps, to say that Washington was a very modest man who paid fastidious attention to his hair, teeth, and attire. Washington understood the importance of how he was perceived by all those around him. He believed staunchly, for instance, that "clothes help make the man." But there is an enormous difference between strutting around like a peacock and maintaining a dignified, handsome appearance and always dressing appropriately for the occasion.

It's called "class," and George Washington had it in spades.

He designed many of his own uniforms, and he certainly knew how to wear one with confidence and style. There is no question that Washington knew the power of presentation, and he strove for a notable image from a very young age. He was also unwavering in his insistence on certain standards for his soldiers. Here Washington instructs on how to maintain a "fine Regiment" and extols the virtues of cleanliness, order, and pride:

The true distinction, Sir, between what is called a fine Regiment, and an indifferent one, will ever, upon investigation, be found to originate in, and depend upon the care, or the inattention, of the Officers belonging to them. Who will see that the Soldiers Clothes are well made, kept whole, and Clean. Those Officers I say who attend to these things, and their duty strictly enjoins it on them, [give health, comfort, and a Military pride to their Men] which fires and fits them for everything great and noble. It is by this means the character of a Regiment is exalted, while Sloth inattention and neglect produce the reverse of these in every particular and must infallibly lessen the reputation of the Corps.[1]

As general and president, Washington faced a difficult balancing act. He believed that a certain level of pomp and circumstance was necessary to establish an image of strength and importance, and to send a signal to foreign nations that America was prepared to take its proper place in the hierarchy of nations. The people were also accustomed to leaders who carried themselves with an air of confidence and entitlement, and pride in this leader translated into pride in their nation and themselves. Yet Washington also knew that a great deal of blood had been shed to push a king aside, so the new republican leader needed to eschew behaviors that would be interpreted as royal. Washington walked this tightrope with great aplomb.

Titles Really Do Matter   As the war against His Majesty, King George III got under way, what title did Americans bestow upon their new commander in chief? Surprisingly, their choice was "His Excellency," which Washington adopted without raising an eyebrow. Both the political leaders of the revolution and Washington himself understood that the people needed a figurehead with an appropriately lofty title to go head-to-head with George III. So they ignored the royal overtones and placed Washington on a pedestal—still far beneath a throne, of course, but high enough to provide a source of inspiration and confidence.

Learning Civility   Many of the principles in the *Rules of Civility* (see Part II) do not focus on issues of morality and character but rather on the social graces. Washington knew that how he looked and behaved would be important ingredients in his success, no matter which course his career took. Learning to dine, dance, and converse were high priorities for the young Washington, and his social skills served him well throughout his life.

The Dancer   As we've seen, Washington paid for his own dance lessons when he was 14 or 15; not only was he a quick learner, but he nurtured his dancing skills throughout his life. During the Revolutionary War, Washington apparently danced with Kitty Greene, the wife of General Nathanael Greene, for three hours straight. When he was president, Mrs. Washington sometimes had to greet guests at the door because there was a queue of ladies waiting for a spin around the dance floor with her husband. As one onlooker noted, all the ladies were eager "to get a touch of him."

Dr. Washington   Washington always felt that his education had been inadequate, and when compared with the formal schooling of some of his contemporaries—Jefferson, Adams and many others—it was. Thus, it is not surprising, consid ering his awareness of his public persona, that Washing accepted honorary degrees awarded to him by five o most prestigious institutions of higher learning of the Washington received LLDs (doctor of law degree

Harvard (1776), Yale (1781), University of Pennsylvania (1783), Washington College (1789), and Brown (1790).

Perception Is Reality   During several periods in his life, Washington found himself short of cash, often because of his extensive real estate investments. Yet he knew it was vital to maintain a certain standard of living. In a 1769 letter to George Mason, Washington wrote that it was difficult to economize because "such an alteration in the system of my living will create suspicions of a decay in my fortune and such a thought the world must not harbor."[2] Washington knew that his standing as a leader in business and society might be irreparably harmed if people perceived that his wealth had diminished and that he had been forced to cut corners. Like modern businesspeople, Washington knew that his reputation must be safeguarded for long-term success. He did not spend wildly—it was not in Washington's nature even during good times—but he did spend the money required to keep up appearances.

A Standing of Perfect Equality   Regarding Washington's presentation of the new nation to the world at large, Daniel Webster said:

> [H]e maintained true dignity and unsullied honor in all communications with foreign states. It was among the high duties devolved upon him, to introduce our new government into the circle of civilized states and powerful nations. Not arrogant or assuming, with no unbecoming or supercilious bearing, he yet exacted for it from all others entire and punctilious respect. *He demanded, and he obtained at once, a standing of per-* *equality for his country in the society of nations;* nor there a prince or potentate of his day, whose nal character carried with it, into the inter-

course of other states, a greater degree of respect and veneration.[3]

Washington dealt with foreign leaders as an equal, and he recognized how critical it was to act like a world leader, each and every day.

The Politics of Surrender   The day after the monumental British defeat at Yorktown—the battle that sealed the fate of the Revolutionary War—a surrender ceremony was scheduled for 2:00 P.M., complete with the ritual stacking of the defeated army's weapons and the surrender of Cornwallis's sword to Washington. Apparently Cornwallis was so humiliated by his crushing defeat that he feigned illness and sent a deputy in his place to turn over the sword.

Washington, however, refused to accept his enemy's sword from a substitute, and the sword was taken, instead, by General Benjamin Lincoln.

Was this Washington's pride revealing itself—or was he sending a not-so-subtle signal that America intended to be England's equal and most certainly not a second-rate player on the world stage?

Military protocol was specific: Neither the leader of the French forces, Rochambeau, nor Washington himself should accept the surrender of a sword from someone beneath their rank. And neither man did.

But Washington unquestionably understood the greater significance of this decision. At that moment, he made it clear to Britain and the world that the United States intended to be equal to any other nation on earth.

Always in Charge   Washington loved the theater, and of his favorite plays was *Cato* by Joseph Addison. A hardly popular today, the play is a classic lesson leadership.

Washington's "performance" at Newburgh (see Leadership Lesson #11), during which he convinced his recalcitrant men to remain loyal to the civilian government, is a powerful example of the knowledge and talent of someone who knows his audience and can take charge of a room. In all likelihood, Washington recalled Cato's scolding rebuke: "Hence, worthless men! hence! . . . You could not undergo the toils of war, Nor bear the hardships that your leader bore."[4] But Washington decided that scolding was not the best approach to take with his men. Instead, he called upon their deep-rooted patriotism and love of country. He didn't scream his message, but rather drew his men together, in the most intimate fashion, treating them as a band of brothers, not lowly subordinates.

Washington instinctively knew—as did Lincoln later—that appealing to the spirit, through emotion and passion, was often more effective than reason and logic.

Appearance Counts!   Washington spent considerable time and money on his false teeth, with less-than-spectacular results. The finished dentures were so clumsy and awkward that they were used for appearance only—he really could not chew food or talk properly with his dentures in place! Yet he doggedly wore them so his face would appear stronger and more normal. He understood he needed to look the part, and endured significant discomfort to do so.

Fiercest among the Savages!   Among the best physical descriptions of Washington is that in *Travels Through the States of North America* by Isaac Weld, Jr., who remembers the reactions the period's most famous artist:

. Mr. Stewart [Gilbert Stuart], the eminent portrait ter, told me, that there are features in his [George ington's] face totally different from what he

ever observed in that of any other human being. . . .
All his features, he observed, were indicative of the
strongest and most ungovernable passions, and had he
been born in the forests, it was his [Stuart's] opinion
that he would have been the fiercest man amongst the
savage tribes. . . . for although General Washington
has been extolled for his great moderation and calm-
ness, during the very trying situations in which he
has so often been placed, yet those who have been
acquainted with him the longest and most intimately
say, that he is by nature a man of a fierce and irritable
disposition; but that, like Socrates, his judgment and
great self-command have always made him appear a
man of a different cast in the eyes of the world.[5]

In essence, Stuart is saying that Washington controlled his
entire presentation to the outside world—and with great
success.

Actions Speak Louder   When Washington first went to the
Virginia legislature, he was known for being incredibly
quiet—he hardly uttered a word. He became known as a good
listener, however, as well as a thoughtful and judicious thinker,
all because he put into practice another of his strongest leadership traits—humility. Throughout his life, in fact, Washington listened far more than he talked. He did not need to
hear the sound of his own voice.

Dress for Success   When Washington attended the Second
Continental Congress in 1775, he selected for his attire the
uniform he had last worn in the French and Indian War.
was the only one to attend wearing the garb of a soldi
clearly it made quite an impression. His attire was far
effective than any speech—it emphasized that he

logical choice to lead the Continental Army in their noble cause.

Summoning Respect   On his way to his inauguration, Washington was feted at a series of public celebrations, at festive dinner parties, and by gushing tributes to the president-elect. Washington was probably embarrassed by all of this attention, but he knew it played an essential role in bringing together the nation. He fully understood that he was the living, breathing embodiment of this new experiment in self-government, and the more excitement his inauguration could generate, the better. By the time he took the oath of office, a great percentage of Americans were already engaged in the new federal government—and they felt a part of it. Washington clearly recognized the public relations aspect of his job, and he played it to the hilt. Today, a CEO who can generate enthusiasm for his or her administration—and make people feel they are a part of it—has half the battle won.

Counterpoint: *Red Means Dead*

Washington was also shrewd enough to know when appearance must be subordinate to security and safety. In May 1777, Washington wrote a stern letter to his Clothier General, James Mease, instructing him to immediately cease the practice of Continental Army soldiers wearing red: "Being more and more convinced, of the impolicy of any part of our Troops being Clothed in Red and that many injurious and fatal consequences are to be apprehended from it, I think it necessary to repeat my request, mentioned in my last, that you will have all the Clothes in your hands, of that Colour, dyed of some other, as soon as you can. . . . Unless the matter is immediately remedied, by changing the Colour, our people will be destroying themselves."[6]

Leadership Lesson 14

∿

A Leader Exceeds Expectations

High expectations are the key to everything.

—SAM WALTON

*I*n an essay titled "A Foot in the Door" in *Mechanical Engineering* magazine, human resources expert Ron Rorrer talks about the challenge of motivating employees to go above and beyond. In the typical employee review process, "exceeds expectations" is usually the highest performance rating possible. Yet managers know that only 5 percent of their employees will achieve this level of accomplishment. Rorrer's bottom line is that the best employees consciously *practice* exceeding expectations, not just now and then, but every single day. They deliberately overachieve. They consider the position's job description as a starting point, not the end-all of an employee's performance.[1]

George Washington rarely promised more than he could deliver, and such reliability and dependability—yet again, *confidence and trust*—were key to his growing popularity among the American people. Over time, Americans almost routine setthe bar higher when it came to General Washington, a later, President Washington. His successes, along with employment of the many leadership traits we've discuss this volume, elevated Washington in the eyes of the people to almost divine status.

Yet Washington himself was often wracked with self-doubt. Although he was very careful in how he communicated this to others, Washington was sometimes much less certain that he could achieve his country's goals than were the people whom he led.

Thus, the ironic duality of Washington's personality: His accomplishments led to high expectations, but it was his humility and self-effacement that helped him to achieve things he himself doubted were possible.

Against All Odds   It was common knowledge—and the common wisdom—that the Revolutionary War was an "against all odds" situation. The American army was far out-manned, outtrained, and outmanaged. The British army was the most powerful in the world. And it was supported by one of the wealthiest nations on earth, plentifully supplied with munitions and foodstuffs. Against all odds, indeed.

In 1775, in one of the three surviving letters of Washington to his wife, Martha, he wrote as he accepted the role of commander in chief that the position was "a trust too far great for my capacity."[2] But he then noted that it would be dishonorable to refuse the commission. He also told her that he had drafted a will—not exactly the encouraging words a wife wants to hear! In effect, Washington was beginning the war by clearly stating that it might not be possible to win it—try as he might—and that he would in all likelihood die in the trying.

Interestingly, Washington expressed a similar sentiment to is mother in 1755 when he wrote to tell her he would be ing command of the Virginia Regiment in the French and an War: "If it is in my power to avoid going to the Ohio , I shall, but if the Command is press'd upon me by the genl. voice of the Country, and offer'd upon such terms as can't be objected against, it wou'd reflect eternal dishonour upon me to refuse it . . ."[3]

Of course, Washington's doubts were ultimately proven wrong in both wars. With the help of the colonists, the mighty British defeated the French to gain supremacy in North America. Twenty years later, George Washington transformed the ragtag colonials into a real fighting force, and the British were sent packing. He proved to be America's secret weapon.

Education Is the Future . . . and Washington Knew It

On January 29, 1769, Washington sent a letter to his friend William Ramsay informing him that he would pay the tuition of £25 per year for Ramsay's son William to attend Jersey College.

Washington freely extended this generosity and benevolence because he had been told that the Ramsay boy was "a youth fond of study and instruction, and disposed to a . . . studious life; in following of which he may not only promote his own happiness, but the future welfare of others."[4]

Washington took the lead in voluntarily assisting someone who might, ultimately, help others. This kind of positive foresight and kindness was certainly more than either his friend or his son could have expected of the great man. Yet Washington considered it almost a duty—a contribution to his friend and his nation.

The Happiness of His People

Washington knew that ː free society, the people's will should be paramount. He knew that throughout history, monarchs often invert mandate and strove only to amass ever larger fort themselves.

In 1788, Washington expressed this thought iː

his dear friend the Marquis de Lafayette, subtly addressing the vast disparity in their respective forms of government. Washington was preaching to the choir, of course, since Lafayette had distinguished himself during the Revolutionary War, fighting on the side of the Americans. Later he was an early supporter of the monarchy-busting French Revolution. Washington was very close to Lafayette—as we have seen, they had a father-son type of relationship—so he felt comfortable discussing what was a potentially controversial issue.

He wrote, "It is a wonder to me, there should be found a single monarch, who does not realize that his own glory and felicity must depend on the prosperity and happiness of his People. How easy is it for a sovereign to do that which shall not only immortalize his name, but attract the blessings of millions."[5]

Genuinely modest, Washington always tried to downplay his own abilities and make it clear that he might not be up to a challenge. His goal was to exceed the sometimes cynical expectations of the populace. What makes this action important, however, is not simply that it worked, but that it was genuine. Washington did not develop this strategy to gain personal wealth or power. He did indeed exceed all expectations by making the right decisions for the right reasons.

Inauguration of Washington, engraving published by Johnson, Fry & Co., after painting by Alonzo Chappel, 1859

Washington's foresight was universal, long-term, and wise, and in his inaugural address he spoke of the "eternal rules of order and right."

Washington Presiding in the Convention of 1787, engraved by John Rogers c.1850s

One of Washington's most heartfelt wishes was for history to remember him as "an honest man" and his stellar reputation inspired his peers to put their trust in him to helm the 1787 Constitutional Convention.

All illustrations were provided by the Mount Vernon Ladies' Association.

Courtship of Washington, engraving by John C. McRae, 1860

Washington was notably ambitious, both in love and war, and his marriage to Martha elevated his stature in Virginia aristocracy.

Washington Crossing the Allegheny, Daniel Huntington, attributed c.1850s

Washington's courage was epic in scope and he faced challenges fearlessly and with determination. Here, he crosses the Allegheny River in the dead of winter on a roughly built raft.

Washington before Princeton, Charles Wilson Peale, 1780

Washington was always in control of his emotions, no matter what the situation, and he was known for his stoic, dignified bearing. This Peale portrait depicts a bold and confident Washington at the 1777 Battle of Princeton.

PUBLISHED BY CURRIER & IVES.   Entered according to act of Congress in the year 1876 by Currier & Ives, in the Office of the Librarian of Congress at Washington.   185 NASSAU ST. NEW YORK.

WASHINGTON TAKING COMMAND OF THE AMERICAN ARMY.
At Cambridge, Mass. July 3rd 1775.

Washington Taking Command of the American Army, July 3rd, 1775, published by Currier and Ives, 1876

Washington verily lived the motto "the buck stops here," and he always took personal responsibility when required. Here, Washington personally takes command of the Continental Army.

COLONEL GEORGE WASHINGTON
6 1732 – 1799 3
Foxhunter

Colonel George Washington, Fox Hunter, engraved by R.L. Boyer, 1931

Washington's determination—his unwavering resolve—was one of his most profound virtues no matter what task he tackled. In this 1857 portrait, he is seen at the age when he was a passionate fox hunter.

Washington at Mount Vernon 1797, lithograph published by N. Currier, 1852

Washington worked hard his entire life, beginning at a very early age and continuing until the very week he died. Here he is seen on horseback overseeing the work in his fields.

Washington at the Battle of Princeton (detail), engraver unknown, 1857

Washington's judgement was motivated by his devotion to his country and his desire to always work for the greater good. This painting depicts Washington rallying his troops at the Battle of Princeton, ultimately winning the encounter that eliminated the British presence from New Jersey.

Battle of Monongahela, July 9, 1755, **lithograph by Claude Regnier, after a painting by Junius Brutus Stearns, 1854**

Washington learned from his mistakes. After assuming command at the 1755 Battle of Monongahela and ending up on the losing side, he pondered his and Braddock's defeat and applied the lessons to his future military strategies.

Washington's Farewell to his Officers, engraved by Thomas
Phillibrowne after Chappel, 1858

Washington was a leader who was loved by his troops, his colleagues,
and his country. This painting portrays the humble general personally
thanking his men.

The Life George Washington: The Farmer, engraved by Claude
Regnier after a painting by Junius Brutus Stearns, 1853

This painting portrays Washington as businessman and farmer. He was
actively involved in both the financial and agricultural decisions made
at Mount Vernon.

A Presidential Reception in 1789, **published by Currier and Ives, 1876**

George Washington understood the meaning—and value—of a dignified, impressive presentation. Here he is seen with Martha at a 1789 reception in his honor.

Washington Crossing the Delaware, **engraved by Paul Girardet, after Emanuel Gottlieb Leutze, 1853**

Washington's night crossing of the Delaware during a blizzard was a seemingly impossible task, yet the General exceeded everyone's expectations by successfully making the trip and then going on to win the Battle of Trenton.

The Prayer at Valley Forge, engraved by John C. McRae, 1889

Faith in a higher power—what Washington often described as Divine Providence—was a powerful force in his life. This painting shows Washington in prayer at Valley Forge.

Mount Vernon, photograph by Robert C. Lautman

George Washington's beloved Mount Vernon, the place he longed for during his many years away from home.

Leadership Lesson 15

~

A Leader Has Heartfelt Faith

Faith consists in believing when it is beyond the power of reason to believe.

—VOLTAIRE

*T*here are two types of faith: secular and religious.

Secular faith is a willingness to believe that something is possible, whether it be a business endeavor or a personal achievement. This kind of faith reflects a stick-to-it attitude, accompanied by a certainty that something can be done, regardless of the obstacles or odds against it happening.

Religious faith is the belief in a higher power—of some sort. Whether exercised through the structure of an organized religion or through personal prayer and devotion, religious faith first and foremost embraces the idea of God.

Clearly, George Washington possessed both types of faith. In this volume, we have referred to his secular faith time and time again—he believed strongly that good people could accomplish great things. When it comes to religious faith, however, Washington's feelings are less obvious. That's why so many scholars avoid the issue entirely.

Washington's favorite word for God was "Providence," and he used the term with great frequency and in a very public manner. Many scholars point out that he seldom mentions "Jesus," "Christ," or "Jesus Christ" in his writings.[1] This is true. But on many occasions, Washington gave Providence credit for the success of the American army. In essence, he felt that Americans were good people with a worthy cause, who were blessed with the assistance of a higher power.

In his November 27, 1783, letter to the members of the Reformed German Congregation of New York, he wrote, "Disposed, at every suitable opportunity to acknowledge publicly our infinite obligations to the Supreme Ruler of the Universe for rescuing our Country from the brink of destruction; I cannot fail at this time to ascribe all the honor of our late successes to the same glorious Being."[2]

For generations, historians have brushed over the role that religion played in Washington's life. Many scholars describe Washington as a deist. This means, in most circles, that God created the world with all of its complexities. But this God takes a step back and just watches. He refuses to intervene.

Several recent books, however (especially Michael and Jana Novak's *Washington's God* and Peter Lillback's *George Washington's Sacred Fire*), have made convincing arguments—at least to me—that the term "deist" doesn't go far enough, that Washington was far more religious than he has generally been given credit for, and that he strongly believed that religion played an important role in American society.

His silence on specific tenets of Christianity aside, Washington felt that an effective government must be populated by leaders (and citizens) who share strong morals and well-defined values. Formal religion nurtures this morality and value system, so it is not merely a "nice thing," but also a necessary aspect of a successful nation.

It is undeniable that Washington used both secular faith and religious doctrine as leadership tools, generally in an effective manner.

Giving God Credit Although Washington deserves to be credited as the indispensable man during the War of Independence, he himself ascribed the country's success to God on more than one occasion:

> When I contemplate the interposition of Providence, as it was visibly manifested, in guiding us through the Revolution . . . I feel myself . . . almost overwhelmed with a sense of the divine munificence . . .[3]

> The kind interposition of Providence which has been so often manifested in the affairs of this country, must naturally lead us to look up to that divine source for light and direction in this new and untried Scene.[4]

> Providence has heretofore taken us up when all other means and hope seemed to be departing from us . . .[5]

> If such talents as I possess have been called into action by great events, and those events have terminated happily for our country, the glory should be ascribed to the manifest interposition of an overruling Providence.[6]

> I was but the humble Agent of favouring Heaven, whose benign interference was so often manifested in our behalf, and to whom the praise of victory alone is due.[7]

Divine Smiles Washington believed wholeheartedly in religious freedom, and during his first term as president, he corresponded with great feeling and enthusiasm with the Hebrew Congregation in Newport, Rhode Island, providing a sensitive and meaningful testimony to the importance of religious tolerance. "For happily the Government of the United States . . . gives to bigotry no sanction, to persecution no assistance."[8]

In a letter to the clergy of Newport, Washington attributes the success of his "weak but honest endeavors" to the "smiles of divine Providence," and states that the "same benignant influence" will be necessary for him to be useful to the people over whom he was called to preside.[9]

To modern ears, the term "religious freedom" too often translates into an *absence* of religion, and a banishment of all mention of God in public discourse. When voices are ostensibly speaking on the government's behalf, religion is considered taboo. But it simply wasn't so in eighteenth-century America, where God was typically part of a soldier's life, and where religion certainly played a role in politics as well. Many members of the founding generation believed in freedom of religion and were very religious men, who felt strongly that some type of religion was a positive influence on individual behavior.

One Nation Washington, two days before the Declaration of Independence proclaimed America free, issued General Orders in which he placed the fragile fate of his nascent nation in the hands of God:

> The time is now near at hand which must probably determine whether Americans are to be freemen or slaves; whether they are to have any property they can call their own. . . . The fate of unborn millions will now depend, under God, on the courage and conduct of this army. . . . Let us therefore rely on the goodness of the cause and the aid of the Supreme Being, in whose hands victory is, to animate and encourage us to great and noble actions.[10]

A Spontaneous Utterance   When George Washington took the oath as first president of the United States in 1789, many people believe that it was his personal decision to add the phrase "So help me God," which was not part of the original oath. The phrase is still used today by Americans taking public office and in other legal proceedings.

Knowing What's Proper   It is hard to know with certainty what was going through the minds of those who read Washington's first inaugural address. But we can be fairly certain that, considering the tenor of the times, people expected a reference to God. And Washington did not disappoint. He openly acknowledged the new country's dependence on God: "It would be peculiarly improper," he declared, "to omit in this first official Act, my fervent supplications to that Almighty Being who rules over the Universe, who presides in the Council of Nations, and whose providential aids can supply every human defect, that his benediction may consecrate to the liberties and happiness of the People of the United States."[11]

Washington was specific and vocal about the power of faith, the value of religion, and his resolute insistence on religious tolerance for all. Here is a sampling of Washington's comments on religion in which he exercises leadership based on his personal faith.

No America without God's help:

Although guided by our excellent Constitution in the discharge of official duties, and actuated, through the whole course of my public life, solely by a wish to promote the best interests of our country; yet, without the beneficial interposition of the Supreme Ruler of the Universe, we could not have reached the distinguished situation which we have attained with such unprecedented rapidity. To him, therefore,

*should we bow with gratitude and reverence, and endeavor to
merit a continuance of his special favors.*
    —George Washington to the General Assembly
        of Rhode Island, April 3, 1797

Religious duties of nations:
*It is the duty of all nations to acknowledge the providence of
Almighty God, to obey His will, to be grateful for His ben-
efits, and to humbly implore His protection and favor.*
    —Thanksgiving Proclamation, October 3, 1789

Morality as a source of the nation's happiness:
*While I reiterate the professions of my dependence upon
Heaven as the source of all public and private blessings; I will
observe that the general prevalence of piety, philanthropy,
honesty, industry, and economy seems, in the ordinary course
of human affairs, particularly necessary for advancing and
confirming the happiness of our country. While all men
within our territories are protected in worshipping the Deity
according to the dictates of their consciences; it is rationally to
be expected from them in return, that they will be emulous
of evincing the sanctity of their professions by the innocence
of their lives and the beneficence of their actions; for no man,
who is profligate in his morals, or a bad member of the civil
community, can possibly be a true Christian, or a credit to
his own religious society.*
    —Letter to Caleb Gibbs, May 26, 1789

No religious arguments, please:
*Of all the animosities which have existed among mankind,
those which are caused by a difference of sentiments in religion appear to be the most inveterate and distressing, and
ought most to be deprecated.*
    —Letter to Edward Newenham, October 20, 1792

Respect by soldiers for all religions:

> *I also give it in Charge to you to avoid all Disrespect to or Contempt of the Religion of the Country and its Ceremonies. Prudence, Policy, and a true Christian Spirit, will lead us to look with Compassion upon their Errors without insulting them. While we are contending for our own Liberty, we should be very cautious of violating the Rights of Conscience in others, ever considering that God alone is the Judge of the Hearts of Men, and to him only in this Case, they are answerable.*
>
> —*Letter to Benedict Arnold, September 14, 1775*

The definitive expression of religious freedom:

> *I have often expressed my sentiments, that every man, conducting himself as a good citizen, and being accountable to God alone for his religious opinions, ought to be protected in worshipping the Deity according to the dictates of his own conscience.*
>
> —*Letter to the General Committee of the United Baptist Churches in Virginia, May, 1789*

PART II

❀

The Rules of Civility

When once the forms of civility are violated, there remains little hope of return to kindness or decency.

—SAMUEL JOHNSON

Be civil to all, sociable to many, familiar with few, friend to one, enemy to none.

—BENJAMIN FRANKLIN

Sometime before he turned 16, as an exercise, George Washington wrote out by hand 110 "Rules of Civility & Decent Behavior in Company and Conversation"— a list of instructions found in a book called *Youths Behavior, or Decency in Conversation Amongst Men,* by Francis Hawkins. Hawkins, at the age of eight, had translated from French a sixteenth-century text used by the Jesuits to shape the moral ethos of young men.

These precepts focused on morality, ethics, codes of conduct, respect, dignity, and honor, as well as matters of etiquette and dining habits. Historian Richard Brookhiser, in his introduction to *Rules of Civility: The*

110 Precepts That Guided Our First President in War and Peace, notes that these maxims "seek to form the inner man . . . by shaping the outer."

These rules had a great impact on the young George Washington, and their universality has application today. In this section we will look at how certain rules of civility by which Washington lived his entire life can be reinterpreted and applied to a modern business, social, cultural, or political paradigm, with cogent examples from the deeds and words of real-world corporate, political, and cultural leaders. Specific rules are annotated with anecdotes and stories of well-known figures both implementing the Washingtonian rules and, unfortunately, sometimes ignoring them.

(NOTE: All original spelling of the rules has been retained.)

The Rules of Civility

❀

Rule 1

*Every Action done in Company, ought to be with Some
Sign of Respect, to those that are Present.*
Or . . .
Know your place in the hierarchy.

The tipping point. Italian entrepreneur Amadeo Giannini created the branch banking system and is known
for his determination and resolve in refusing to allow
his bank's assets to be destroyed during the 1906 San
Francisco earthquake.

One day, in the time after Giannini's Bank of America
had grown to become the largest privately owned bank
in the world, Amadeo was standing on the sidewalk next
to a distinguished gentleman with gray hair. Giannini
respectfully asked the man to hail him a taxicab. The
man immediately did as Giannini asked, and the banker

thanked him . . . and then handed him a quarter as a tip.

The man bristled and coolly informed Giannini that he was the president of the Los Angeles Bank of America. The man worked for Giannini! The Italian banker immediately apologized for his seeming act of disrespect and took back the quarter, but then handed the man a dollar instead.

In this situation, Giannini showed respect to the man by apologizing for tipping someone of such high standing, an inadvertently insulting gesture. But then Giannini turned the rule on its ear by quadrupling the tip, subtly reminding the man of his own authority and, in a sense, demeaning him by the unspoken message "Yes, you deserve respect for your position, but you are still inferior to me and subject to my beneficence."

The proper response by the gray-haired gentleman—who most certainly knew who Giannini was—should have been to graciously accept the quarter and make no effort to assert his importance to someone in a position of authority superior to his.

Humility should have trumped pride and self-importance, but it did not, and thus the man was subjected to a humiliating, symbolic scolding.

❀

2d *When in Company, put not your Hands to any Part of the Body, not usualy Discovered.*

3d *Shew Nothing to your Freind that may affright him.*

4th *In the Presence of Others Sing not to yourself with a humming Noise, nor Drum with your Fingers or Feet.*

5th *If You Cough, Sneeze, Sigh, or Yawn, do it not Loud but Privately; and Speak not in your Yawning, but put Your handkercheif or Hand before your face and turn aside.*

6th *Sleep not when others Speak, Sit not when others stand, Speak not when you Should hold your Peace, walk not on when others Stop.*

7th *Put not off your Cloths in the presence of Others, nor go out your Chamber half Drest.*

8th *At Play and at Fire its Good manners to Give Place to the last Commer, and affect not to Speak Louder than Ordinary.*

9th *Spit not in the Fire, nor Stoop low before it neither Put your Hands into the Flames to warm them, nor Set your Feet upon the Fire especially if there be meat before it.*

10th *When you Sit down, Keep your Feet firm and Even, without putting one on the other or Crossing them.*

11th *Shift not yourself in the Sight of others nor Gnaw your nails.*

12th *Shake not the head, Feet, or Legs rowl not the Eys lift not one eyebrow higher than the other wry not the mouth, and bedew no mans face with your Spittle, by approaching too near him when you Speak.*

13th *Kill no Vermin as Fleas, lice ticks &c in the Sight of Others, if you See any filth or thick Spittle put your foot Dexteriously upon it if it be upon the Cloths of your Companions, Put it off privately, and if it be upon your own Cloths return Thanks to him who puts it off.*

14th *Turn not your Back to others especially in Speaking, Jog not the Table or Desk on which Another reads or writes, lean not upon any one.*

15th *Keep your Nails clean and Short, also your Hands and Teeth Clean yet without Shewing any great Concern for them.*

16th *Do not Puff up the Cheeks, Loll not out the tongue rub the Hands, or beard, thrust out the lips, or bite them or keep the Lips too open or too Close.*

17th *Be no Flatterer, neither Play with any that delights not to be Play'd Withal.*

18th *Read no Letters, Books, or Papers in Company but when there is a Necessity for the doing of it you must ask leave: come not near the Books or Writings of Another so as to read them unless desired or give your opinion of them unask'd also look not nigh when another is writing a Letter.*

Early to rise . . .   Washington was an avid reader and a prolific letter writer, yet the ceaseless parade of family members, guests, and visitors at Mount Vernon often made it difficult for him to find the time and privacy to accommodate these pursuits. How did Washington abide by Rule 18? He rose very early every morning and sequestered himself in his office, working steadily until breakfast. (And many mornings he actually rode on horseback to his different farms, to be sure that others were hard at work, too.) Better to lose a little sleep than be rude.

❁

19th *Let your Countenance be pleasant but in Serious Matters Somewhat grave.*

20th *The Gestures of the Body must be Suited to the discourse you are upon.*

21st *Reproach none for the Infirmaties of Nature, nor Delight to Put them that have in mind thereof.*

22d *Shew not yourself glad at the Misfortune of another though he were your enemy.*

23d *When you see a Crime punished, you may be inwardly Pleased; but always shew Pity to the Suffering Offender.*

The higher ground ... During the Revolutionary War, General Washington insisted that all British prisoners be treated humanely and with respect—even though the British deliberately exercised what one British officer described as "every species of barbarity" against both American soldiers and civilians.

❁

24th *Do not laugh too loud or too much at any Publick Spectacle.*

25th *Superfluous Complements and all Affectation of Ceremonie are to be avoided, yet where due they are not to be Neglected.*

26th *In Pulling off your Hat to Persons of Distinction, as Noblemen, Justices, Churchmen &c make a Reverence, bowing more or less according to the Custom of the Better Bred, and Quality of the Person. Amongst your equals expect not always that they Should begin with you first, but to Pull off the Hat when there is no need is Affectation, in the Manner of Saluting and resaluting in words keep to the most usual Custom.*

27th *Tis ill manners to bid one more eminent than yourself be covered as well as not to do it to whom it's due Likewise he that makes too much haste to Put on his hat does not well, yet he ought to Put it on at the first, or at most the Second time of being ask'd; now what is herein Spoken, of Qualification in behaviour in Saluting, ought also to be observed in taking of Place, and Sitting down for ceremonies without Bounds is troublesome.*

28th *If any one come to Speak to you while you are Sitting Stand up tho he be your Inferiour, and when you Present Seats let it be to every one according to his Degree.*

29th *When you meet with one of Greater Quality than yourself, Stop, and retire especially if it be at a Door or any Straight place to give way for him to Pass.*

30th *In walking the highest Place in most Countrys Seems to be on the right hand therefore Place yourself on the left of him whom you desire to Honour: but if three walk together the middest Place is the most Honourable the wall is usually given to the most worthy if two walk together.*

31st *If any one far Surpasses others, either in age, Estate, or Merit yet would give Place to a meaner than himself in his own lodging or elsewhere the one ought not to except it, So he on the other part should not use much earnestness nor offer it above once or twice.*

32d *To one that is your equal, or not much inferior you are to give the cheif Place in your Lodging and he to who 'tis offered ought at the first to refuse it but at the Second to accept though not without acknowledging his own unworthiness.*

33d *They that are in Dignity or in office have in all places Preceedency but whilst they are Young they ought to respect those that are their equals in Birth or other Qualitys, though they have no Publick charge.*

34th *It is good Manners to prefer them to whom we Speak before ourselves especially if they be above us with whom in no Sort we ought to begin.*

35th *Let your Discourse with Men of Business be Short and Comprehensive.*

To the point . . . George Washington was known for his taciturn manner. He often remained silent as others spoke, choosing to weigh in when it was judicious and appropriate.

❀

36th *Artificers & Persons of low Degree ought not to use many ceremonies to Lords, or Others of high Degree but Respect and highly Honour them, and those of high Degree ought to treat them with affibility & Courtesie, without Arrogancy.*

37th *In Speaking to men of Quality do not lean nor Look them full in the Face, nor approach too near them at lest Keep a full Pace from them.*

38th *In visiting the Sick, do not Presently play the*
Physicion if you be not Knowing therein.

❀

Rule 39

In writing or Speaking, give to every Person his due
Title According to his Degree & the Custom of the Place.
Or . . .
Be polite. At all times.

Spontaneously polite . . . George Washington seldom
proclaimed his superiority, nor did he seek acclaim. In
fact, he shunned it. He was always respectful and deferential to whomever he was speaking, whether it was
French nobility or the humblest farmer or lowest-
ranking soldier. He knew his place in the hierarchy: He
was commander in chief, and then president, but his
innate humility and respect for others summoned from
him a mien that caused one visiting Frenchman to
remark, "I have never seen anyone who was more natu-
rally and spontaneously polite."[1]

❀

Rule 40

Strive not with your Superiors in argument, but always
Submit your Judgment to others with Modesty.
Or . . .
State your case with dignity.

Respectfully submitted . . . In the late 1970s, Chrysler chairman Lee Iacocca proved to the federal government that if his car company were allowed to fail (which it was perilously close to doing), then the nation's unemployment rate would go up one half of 1 percent overnight, tens of thousands of jobs would be lost to the Japanese (the only manufacturers who were readily able to supply the small cars Americans wanted), and the country's free market system would lose a major competitor if Chrysler was not around to offer and sell over 1 million vehicles a year.

Iacocca also brought into the argument the Treasury Department's estimate that if Chrysler failed, it would cost the United States $2.7 billion in the first year alone due to unemployment benefits and welfare payments.

Lee Iacocca's calm, reasoned, logical, *dispassionate* argument that the federal government should guarantee $1.2 billion in loans to his failing company is a classic example of this Washingtonian rule. He did not argue or threaten, he was humble and respectful, but he was committed to making his case to the government and doing everything in his power to see that Chrysler survived—for the good of the company and its employees, yes, but also for the long-term good of the United States.

His personal entreaty worked, and the U.S. government agreed to make the largest federal loan guarantee ever—$1.2 billion—to a single, private company to prevent it from going bankrupt. (Iacocca ultimately repaid the loan in full seven years early.)

❀

Rule 41

Undertake not to Teach your equal in the art himself
Proffesses; it Savours of arrogancy.
Or . . .
Defer to the person who knows what they're doing.

***The cost of experience* . . .** General Electric was having trouble with a complex system of electrical components and equipment, and no one could solve the problem.

The man who had worked on designing both the equipment and the system, electrical engineer Charles Steinmetz, was summoned out of retirement and engaged as a consultant to help solve the problem. Steinmetz dutifully arrived at the plant and spent several hours examining equipment, running tests, and pondering the problem. Finally, he walked up to a piece of equipment and made an X in chalk on one small component of the machine. GE's engineers went to work on the component and, sure enough, the problem was found and quickly corrected.

Shortly thereafter, Steinmetz sent GE an invoice for the amount of $10,000. The powers-that-be at the company were furious at what they perceived to be audacious overcharging and price gouging and demanded an itemized invoice from Steinmetz, insisting that he detail everything he did and reveal precisely what he charged for it.

Steinmetz quickly sent in the requested invoice. It read: "Making chalk mark: $1.00. Knowing where to place it: $9,999.00."

Steinmetz knew he brought a very special expertise to the table and that he was more than the equal of the other engineers in the room. So he really was providing a lesson to those around him, and GE should have expected to pay for it accordingly.

❁

42d *Let thy ceremonies in Courtesie be proper to the Dignity of his place with whom thou conversest for it is absurd to act the same with a Clown and a Prince.*

43d *Do not express Joy before one sick or in pain for that contrary Passion will aggravate his Misery.*

❁

Rule 44

When a man does all he can though it Succeeds not well
blame not him that did it.
Or . . .
Mistakes are how we learn.

Doing his job . . .   Robert Wood Johnson, Jr., the founder of Johnson & Johnson, the company known for its bandages and health products, applied this Washingtonian rule with full commitment.

James Burke was Johnson's director of new products in the early years of Johnson & Johnson, and he once developed a product he thought was a surefire winner. He came up with the idea for a chest rub for colds that was applied in the same manner as a stick deodorant. The product was an abysmal failure, and Burke recalled the day he was called to Johnson's office, fully expecting to be fired.

"I understand that your product failed," his boss said.

"Yes, sir, that's true," Burke responded.

"I understand it cost this corporation $865,000," Johnson continued.

"Yes, sir," Burke replied.

Johnson then stood up, walked around his desk with his hand extended and shook Burke's hand with vigor. "I just want to congratulate you," he told the stunned director. "Nothing happens unless people are willing to make decisions, and you can't make decisions without making mistakes."

❁

45th *Being to advise or reprehend any one, consider whether it ought to be in publick or in Private; presently, or at Some other time in what terms to do it & in reproving Shew no Sign of Cholar but do it with all Sweetness and Mildness.*

❁

Rule 46

Take all Admonitions thankfully in what Time or Place Soever given but afterwards not being culpable take a Time & Place convenient to let him know it that gave them.
Or . . .
Don't make a scene . . . even if you're right.

A time and a place . . . On Wednesday, March 29, 2006, Representative Cynthia McKinney, a six-term African-American Democratic congresswoman from Georgia, attempted to enter a Capitol office building by bypassing standard metal detectors and security screening—as all members of Congress are allowed to do. However, she was not wearing her identification pin, and when a Capitol police officer repeatedly called to her to stop, Representative McKinney ignored him and continued walking into the building. The officer then approached the congresswoman and grabbed her arm in an attempt to prevent her from proceeding into the building.

According to reports, Representative McKinney then immediately turned and struck the officer in the chest with her cell phone and later publicly stated that she believed she had been singled out for harassment because of her race.

This incident is a classic example of someone *not* applying a Washingtonian rule to a volatile professional situation. If she had applied Rule 46, Representative McKinney would have immediately done two things.

First, she would have stopped when ordered to by the Capitol police officer, deferring to his authority in that place. The second thing she should have done on the spot is acknowledge the officer's concern, identify herself as a congresswoman, and prove her identity. "Take all admonitions thankfully."

Obviously, Representative McKinney felt (citing the rule again) "not . . . culpable," so she lashed out; instead, she should have saved her accusations, no matter how justified, for later. Her anger over being confronted in such a manner should not have been acted on in public. She should have named "a Time & Place convenient" for a meeting with the officer's superiors in which she could express her outrage and discuss possible policy changes.

❀

47th *Mock not nor Jest at any thing of Importance break no Jest that are Sharp Biting and if you Deliver any thing witty and Pleasent abstain from Laughing there at yourself.*

48th *Wherein you reprove Another be unblameable yourself; for example is more prevalent than Precepts.*

49th *Use no Reproachfull Language against any one neither Curse nor Revile.*

50th *Be not hasty to beleive flying Reports to the Disparagement of any.*

❀

Rule 51

Wear not your Cloths, foul, unript or Dusty but See they be Brush'd once every day at least and take heed that you approach not to any Uncleaness.
Or . . .
Neatness counts!

Dressed to distill . . . In 1857, Jasper "Jack" Daniel inherited a distillery from his stepfather and, by the time he was 13, had learned how to make a whiskey that was hailed at the St. Louis World's Fair as the finest in the world. Today, this whiskey is Jack Daniel's in the square bottle (which he started using in 1895 and which is now the Jack Daniel's trademark design).

In 1867, when Jasper was 21, he came to the realization that his business was a success and that, accordingly, he was a successful businessman. For several years, Jack had dressed in worn and ragged clothes like one of his distillery workers, instead of the company owner.

Recognizing that he needed to look the part, Jack embraced this Washingtonian rule and decided to change his image. One day he went into town and outfitted himself in an expensive suit and tie. He returned to the distillery in splendor and dressed that way for the rest of his life, until his death in 1911 at the age of 65.

❀

52d *In your Apparel be Modest and endeavour to accomodate Nature, rather than to procure Admiration keep to the Fashion of your equals Such as are Civil and orderly with respect to Times and Places.*

Dress for respect . . . George Washington was always very attentive to his attire and appearance, and he dressed properly for both time and circumstance, favoring stylish yet tasteful garb.

❀

53d *Run not in the Streets, neither go too slowly nor with Mouth open go not Shaking yr Arms kick not the earth with yr feet, go not upon the Toes, nor in a Dancing fashion.*

54th Play not the Peacock, looking every where about you, to See if you be well Deck't, if your Shoes fit well if your Stokings sit neatly, and Cloths handsomely.

55th Eat not in the Streets, nor in the House, out of Season.

❀

Rule 56

Associate yourself with Men of good Quality if you Esteem your own Reputation; for 'tis better to be alone than in bad Company.
Or . . .
We are judged by the company we keep.

***How to hire* . . .** Scottish-born steel magnate and philanthropist Andrew Carnegie once suggested that his epitaph read "Here lies a man who was able to surround himself with men far cleverer than himself."

In an example of quintessential CEO behavior, Carnegie knew to surround himself with the best and the brightest, and he allowed his people free rein to use their skills and ideas the best way they knew how.

Some of Carnegie's underlings included Charles Schwab, who went on to become a world-renowned financier, and Henry Frick, the hard-nosed business tycoon who became a multimillionaire coke (a product used in steelmaking) king. Frick is famous for once stating, "There is no secret about success. Success simply calls for hard work, devotion to your business at all times, day and night."

Carnegie's willingness to defer to underlings for the good of the business is a classic illustration of Washingtonian behavior, and is also a model used by U.S. presidents, who put together a cabinet and staff who do their best work under the president's leadership.

❀

57th *In walking up and Down in a House, only with One in Company if he be Greater than yourself, at the first give him the Right hand and Stop not till he does and be not the first that turns, and when you do turn let it be with your face towards him, if he be a Man of Great Quality, walk not with him Cheek by Joul but Somewhat behind him; but yet in Such a Manner that he may easily Speak to you.*

58th *Let your Conversation be without Malice or Envy, for 'tis a Sign of a Tractable and Commendable Nature: And in all Causes of Passion admit Reason to Govern.*

❀

Rule 59

*Never express anything unbecoming, nor Act agst the
Rules Moral before your inferiours.
Or . . .
Take responsibility.*

The buck stops here . . .   U.S. Navy Commander Scott
Waddle was at the helm of the nuclear submarine the
U.S.S. *Greeneville* when the sub surfaced too quickly in
February 2001 and struck a Japanese fishing vessel,
killing nine Japanese tourists.

Commander Waddle embraced and put into action
this Washingtonian rule when he immediately took full
responsibility for the accident and adamantly shifted all
blame away from his crew and onto himself. "I accept
full responsibility and accountability for the actions of
the crew of the [U.S.S.] *Greeneville*," Waddle said in a statement to the media. "I am truly sorry for the loss of life."

A board of inquiry found Waddle guilty of "derelic-
tion of duty" and "negligent husbandry of a vessel," but did not
seek a court-martial because Waddle took full responsibility for the accident and had an exemplary record until
the accident.

❁

60th Be not immodest in urging your Freinds to Discover a Secret.

61st Utter not base and frivilous things amongst grave and Learn'd Men nor very Difficult Questians or Subjects, among the Ignorant or things hard to be believed, Stuff not your Discourse with Sentences amongst your Betters nor Equals.

62d Speak not of doleful Things in a Time of Mirth or at the Table; Speak not of Melancholy Things as Death and Wounds, and if others Mention them Change if you can the Discourse tell not your Dreams, but to your intimate Friend.

63d A Man ought not to value himself of his Atchievements, or rare Qualities of wit; much less of his riches Virtue or Kindred. Or . . . Remain humble and cultivate modesty.

64th Break not a Jest where none take pleasure in mirth Laugh not aloud, nor at all without Occasion, deride no mans Misfortune, tho' there Seem to be Some cause.

65th Speak not injurious Words neither in Jest nor Earnest Scoff at none although they give Occasion.

66th Be not forward but friendly and Courteous; the first to Salute hear and answer & be not Pensive when it's a time to Converse.

❀

Rule 67

Detract not from others neither be excessive
in Commanding.
Or . . .
Eschew the spotlight.

How to visit the president . . . After George W. Bush's 2000 election as president was confirmed, he visited President Clinton at the White House, and his behavior and comments were a model of this George Washington rule.

Even though he was president-elect, he was respectful, deferential, and appreciative of Clinton's invitation. Regardless of his personal feelings about Clinton's behavior in office or his performance as president, Bush showed great respect to both the office of the presidency and to President Clinton himself and did not use the opportunity of the joint meeting (which was, of course, televised around the world) to boost his own administration's agenda or gloat over his ultimate victory over Clinton's party. He was grateful, dignified, and a class act both when in Clinton's presence and during his comments to the media afterward.

Bush made it clear that Bill Clinton was still president, that Bill Clinton was *his* president, and that he would not usurp that role in any way.

❁

68th *Go not thither, where you know not, whether you Shall be Welcome or not. Give not Advice without being Ask'd & when desired do it briefly.*

69th *If two contend together take not the part of either unconstrained; and be not obstinate in your own Opinion, in Things indiferent be of the Major Side.*

70th *Reprehend not the imperfections of others for that belongs to Parents Masters and Superiours.*

71st *Gaze not on the marks or blemishes of Others and ask not how they came. What you may Speak in Secret to your Friend deliver not before others.*

72d *Speak not in an unknown Tongue in Company but in your own Language and that as those of Quality do and not as the Vulgar; Sublime matters treat Seriously.*

73d *Think before you Speak pronounce not imperfectly nor bring out your Words too hastily but orderly & distinctly. Or . . . Watch what you say.*

74th *When Another Speaks be attentive your Self and disturb not the Audience if any hesitate in his Words help him not nor Prompt him without desired, Interrupt him not, nor Answer him till his Speech be ended.*

75th *In the midst of Discourse ask not of what one treateth but if you Perceive any Stop because of your coming you may well intreat him gently to Proceed: If a Person of Quality comes in while your Conversing it's handsome to Repeat what was said before.*

76th *While you are talking, Point not with your Finger at him of Whom you Discourse nor Approach too near him to whom you talk especially to his face.*

77th *Treat with men at fit Times about Business & Whisper not in the Company of Others.*

78th *Make no Comparisons and if any of the Company be Commended for any brave act of Vertue, commend not another for the Same.*

79th *Be not apt to relate News if you know not the truth thereof. In Discoursing of things you Have heard Name not your Author always A Secret Discover not.*

80th *Be not Tedious in Discourse or in reading unless you find the Company pleased therewith.*

81st *Be not Curious to Know the Affairs of Others neither approach those that Speak in Private.*

❀

Rule 82

*Undertake not what you cannot perform but be carefull
to keep your promise.
Or . . .
Keep your word.*

Dancing in the street . . . The legendary business-man Sam Walton was passionate about striving to excite employees about working at Wal-Mart, and he was devoted to boosting worker morale. He believed that happy employees were motivated and productive employees, and he would bend over backward to maintain a positive attitude about the company. One year, Walton made an extraordinary promise. He vowed to all the hundreds of thousands of Wal-Mart employees that if the company exceeded projections for that quarter, he, Sam Walton, founder of the company, would dance the hula on Wall Street.

The workers delivered . . . and so did Sam. In fulfillment of this Washingtonian rule, Sam Walton kept his promise and danced the hula on Wall Street.

❀

Rule 83

*When you deliver a matter do it without passion & with
discretion, however mean the person be you do it too.*
Or . . .
Omit emotion.

Order in the court . . . This Washingtonian rule is seen in action today (in most cases) in America's courtrooms. Ideally, detached and impartial judges do not allow emotion to take over when sentencing criminals found guilty of the most horrific crimes.

Judges try to remain consistent, as well as cool and composed, when meting out punishment. In many cases, this must be difficult and require a truly monumental exercise of self-control. Emotions often run high during victim impact statements and testimony, but most judges remain above it all and act "without passion & with discretion," regardless of their personal feelings about the heinous deeds of which the accused is found guilty.

❀

Rule 84

When your Superiours talk to any Body hearken not neither Speak nor Laugh.
Or . . .
Don't mock the boss.

Parts inventory . . .   During a visit to the Ford automobile plant in Dearborn, Michigan, a man met Henry Ford himself, who also happened to be at the plant that day.

Ford introduced himself and proudly showed the man a car that had just come off the assembly line. He then told the man that the vehicle contained precisely 4,719 parts.

The visitor was very impressed at the depth of Ford's

knowledge, but wanted to check out the facts himself.
He asked a Ford engineer if what he had been told was
correct. The engineer said he had no idea, and that he
couldn't imagine a more useless piece of information.

The engineer violated Rule 84 by being unable to con-
firm what his "superiour" had said. He then compounded
the insult by mocking the fact that his boss even knew
such details.

The fact that the boss was aware of the minutest of
details about his company's products should have served
as an example to the cavalier employee.

A minimum wage pioneer . . .   In 1914, Ford implemented a $5-a-day minimum wage for his autoworkers, a
move some consider his greatest contribution to American
industry, leading the way for equitable pay for all. He
more than doubled the existing $2.34 for a nine-hour shift
wage, which ultimately resulted in more people being able
to buy his cars.

❀

85th *In Company of these of Higher Quality than yourself Speak not til you are ask'd a Question then Stand
upright put of your Hat & Answer in few words.*

86th *In Disputes, be not So Desireous to Overcome as not
to give Liberty to each one to deliver his Opinion and
Submit to the Judgment of the Major Part especially if
they are Judges of the Dispute.*

87th *Let thy carriage be such as becomes a Man Grave
Settled and attentive to that which is spoken. Contradict
not at every turn what others Say.*

88th *Be not tedious in Discourse, make not many Digressigns, nor repeat often the Same manner of Discourse.*

89th *Speak not Evil of the absent for it is unjust.*

90th *Being Set at meat Scratch not neither Spit Cough or blow your Nose except there's a Necessity for it.*

91st *Make no Shew of taking great Delight in your Victuals, Feed not with Greediness; cut your Bread with a Knife, lean not on the Table neither find fault with what you Eat.*

Rule 92

Take no Salt or cut Bread with your Knife Greasy.
Or . . .
Keep your utensils to yourself.

Manners matter . . . This rule needed to be implemented during a time when the availability of utensils was limited and people at table had to be reminded not to use their own implements for serving. When dining in public, people were reminded to be especially careful when serving themselves from a common food plate. Today, family meals are often so abbreviated and informal that table manners sometimes fall by the wayside. Perhaps it's time for parents to reacquaint themselves, and then their children, with Washington's *Rules of Civility*.

❀

93d *Entertaining any one at table it is decent to present him wt. meat, Undertake not to help others undesired by the Master.*

94th *If you Soak bread in the Sauce let it be no more than what you put in your Mouth at a time and blow not your broth at Table but Stay till Cools of it Self.*

95th *Put not your meat to your Mouth with your Knife in your hand neither Spit forth the Stones of any fruit Pye upon a Dish nor Cast anything under the table.*

96th *It's unbecoming to Stoop much to ones Meat Keep your Fingers clean & when foul wipe them on a Corner of your Table Napkin.*

97th *Put not another bit into your Mouth til the former be Swallowed let not your Morsels be too big for the Gowls.*

98th *Drink not nor talk with your mouth full neither Gaze about you while you are a Drinking.*

99th *Drink not too leisurely nor yet too hastily. Before and after Drinking wipe your Lips breath not then or Ever with too Great a Noise, for its uncivil.*

100th *Cleanse not your teeth with the Table Cloth Napkin Fork or Knife but if Others do it let it be done wt. a Pick Tooth.*

101st *Rince not your Mouth in the Presence of Others.*

102d *It is out of use to call upon the Company often to Eat nor need you Drink to others every Time you Drink.*

103d *In Company of your Betters be not longer in eating than they are lay not your Arm but only your hand upon the table.*

104th *It belongs to the Chiefest in Company to unfold his Napkin and fall to Meat first, But he ought then to Begin in time & to Dispatch with Dexterity that the Slowest may have time allowed him.*

105th *Be not Angry at Table whatever happens & if you have reason to be so, Shew it not but on a Chearfull Countenance especially if there be Strangers for Good Humour makes one Dish of Meat a Feast.*

106th *Set not yourself at the upper of the Table but if it Be your Due or that the Master of the house will have it So, Contend not, least you Should Trouble the Company.*

107th *If others talk at Table be attentive but talk not with Meat in your Mouth.*

108th *When you Speak of God or his Atributes, let it be Seriously & wt. Reverence. Honour & Obey your Natural Parents altho they be Poor.*

109th *Let your Recreations be Manfull not Sinfull.*

110th *Labour to keep alive in your Breast that Little Spark of Celestial fire Called Conscience.*

Thank goodness for America that Washington's spark burned so bright for so long!

PART III

George Washington, Entrepreneur

*T*HE RULES OF CIVILITY INCULCATED IN GEORGE Washington core values he used throughout his life in his capacity as a leader of men and the father of a new nation. He likewise used these values in his role as a businessman to conduct his affairs ethically and fairly. He was also farsighted and creative. In this section we look at one of the lesser-known sides of the Father of Our Country.

We can easily conjure up an image of George Washington on horseback, leading our brave soldiers on the battlefields at Princeton or Monmouth.

It is equally easy to imagine Washington in the halls of government, providing leadership at the Constitutional Convention, or mediating an argument between cabinet members.

But Washington the businessman, the entrepreneur, is a figure few Americans have had the pleasure of meeting.

Washington's approach to America's economy is just as interesting, and in many ways, as important, as his approach to the military and politics. From his teenage years on, Washington was unabashedly ambitious in all walks of life. He possessed a physical and mental energy that few could match. He took chances and made numerous mistakes, but he almost never made the same mistake twice. Even during his final years, he could be classified as the best kind of workaholic: a man absolutely determined to find new ways to make his nation, and himself, the best, and usually the wealthiest, they could be.

It is important to keep in mind that George Washington was not born into wealth. Although the Washington family owned a reasonable amount of land, Washington's father died when George was just 11 years old, and young George faced the unfortunate circumstance of being the son of a second wife. His older half-brother Lawrence inherited Mount Vernon, then known as Little Hunting Creek Plantation, and George was left with what today we might describe as a "high-maintenance" mother, as well as three younger brothers and a sister.

Washington tried to join the British navy when he was 15, but his mother was advised that a boy's chances of climbing the ladder of success in the British navy were slim to none. She also wanted her oldest child at home to help with his siblings. He finally escaped her grasp—but certainly not her influence—by becoming a surveyor's assistant at age 16. In all likelihood, Mary Ball Washington realized her son's income would help to support the family.

One of his first surveying assignments, and one of the turning points in his career, was to help chart nearly 1 million acres of western lands that belonged to Thomas, Lord Fairfax, one of the wealthiest and most influential landowners in Virginia. In a matter of months, Washington had learned firsthand of the vast expanses of untouched land that lay to the west, and he formed a close friendship with the Fairfaxes, one of the wealthiest and most remarkable families in America.

What a cornucopia of contrasting experiences Washington could claim by the time he reached his 21st birthday!

He had walked in forests that perhaps no white man had ever seen, and he had danced at the Fairfax home with the most sought-after damsels in the Colonies.

Although it bothered Washington throughout his life that he did not have the opportunity to attend a university, in a much broader sense, his education was wide-ranging, well-rounded, and intense.

So when he assumed complete ownership of the Mount Vernon estate at the age of twenty-nine, Washington was ready and eager to enter the landed gentry of Virginia plantation owners. At the time, Mount Vernon was not considered a major piece of property—just 2,000 acres, with a few small structures. The Mansion was about a third of the size it is today.

Washington began almost immediately to transform the property into a plantation worthy of the leader he hoped to become. Washington's great excitement for expansion and development was also fueled by his marriage to Martha Custis, one of the wealthiest widows in the Colonies.

Yet distractions conspired over the next four decades to pull Washington away from his business ventures.

He repeatedly answered the call of his country—the Revolutionary War, the Constitutional Convention, and then, finally, the presidency.

He always gave his full and utmost attention to the founding of the nation and, in reality, his personal affairs often suffered great losses due to his absence. There's an old southern proverb that says, "The best fertilizer in the world is the footprint of the owner." During the eight years of the Revolutionary War, Washington stepped foot on his beloved farm but 10 days, and it suffered accordingly.

The point is this: Even under the worst of circumstances, Washington proved to be an innovative and often successful business leader who aggressively invested in America's future. If he had been able to devote *all* his time and creativity to business matters, we can only imagine how successful and wealthy he might have become.

In the pages that follow, we will look at five different areas of business that engaged George Washington for major periods of his life:

➤ *Real estate.* The acquisition of property interested Washington from his earliest years, and his surveying background helped to jump-start his extensive investments in land.

➤ *Farming.* If Washington had ever been asked to fill out a job application, there is no doubt he would have entered the word "farmer" in the occupation blank. He considered it an important calling in his life.

➤ *Subsidiary businesses.* Washington also launched a number of additional businesses at Mount Vernon, including an aggressive gristmill operation, an incredibly productive fishing venture, and, in the final years of his life, a groundbreaking distilling operation.

➤ *Animal husbandry.* Breeding animals fascinated Washington, and he always manifested the tremendous patience necessary to selectively breed dozens of generations of animals, often with great success.

➤ *The canal.* What might be described as Washington's most visionary and entrepreneurial venture was a complex canal system on the Potomac, designed to link the rough-and-tumble western territories to the trading centers of the East.

Not all of these efforts succeeded, of course, but setbacks are the hallmark of a true entrepreneur. Washington was not afraid to fail. He loved the competitive environment of the free enterprise system, and he seldom shied away from taking calculated risks. Washington the businessman also shared an essential quality with Washington the soldier and statesman. His business ethics were consistently strong, and his sterling character trumped his blatant ambition, time and time again.

Real Estate: George Washington's Lust for Land

Washington associated real estate with wealth, prestige, and power, and sometimes his lust for land got the better of him. Several historians have argued that Washington's dealings in real estate were not exclusively aboveboard, and by modern standards, some of these accusations may be justified.

It was common practice in the eighteenth century for officers in the military to be rewarded with land holdings. When Washington became a colonel in the Virginia militia at the ripe old age of 23, he knew that his service to the Crown in the French and Indian War would have its risks as well as its rewards.

The mortality rate for young officers who were often at the front of a charge, was relatively high. At the Battle of the Monongahela, Washington was forced to assume command after General Edward Braddock and 63 of his 86 senior officers were killed or wounded. And he did so without hesitation and with characteristic enthusiasm. In his self-serving chronicle of this battle, Washington describes the danger in great detail, noting that two horses were shot from under him and musket balls cut through his clothing in four different places.

Washington was on the losing side of this conflict, but his reputation for bravery and leadership under extreme fire became well-known throughout the colonies. Clearly, he felt that he deserved to be compensated for his performance as well as his risk of life and limb. When it came time to divide the spoils of war—the distribution of western lands to colonial officers—Washington saw to it that he received some of the most valuable acreage. Today, this preferential treatment may appear to border on the unethical, but in Washington's time it was fairly standard practice.

In 1754, Washington began renting 2,126 acres at Mount Vernon from the widow of his older half-brother Lawrence, who had died relatively young from consumption—in all likelihood, tuberculosis.[1] Washington was only 22 years old, and yet he was determined to expand the plantation even before he became its full-fledged owner.

In 1757, Washington purchased 500 acres of land to the north from his neighbor, Sampson Darnell, for £350. That relatively minor transaction proceeded without a hitch.

Three years later, however, Washington discovered that all is fair, not just in love and war, but in real estate as well. Across Little Hunting Creek was a major tract of land that was suitable both for farming and as a base for a potential fishing operation. Washington believed that a handshake with William Clifton had sealed the deal—1,806 acres for £1,150.

Almost overnight, Clifton tried to quash the sale, bemoaning that his wife could not bear to part with the farm. But a letter that survives in the Mount Vernon collection reveals the truth: Clifton had accepted a better offer. Thomas Mason, brother of Bill of Rights author George Mason, had offered Clifton a mere £50 more, so he reneged on his promise to Washington.

Washington was outraged, describing Clifton as a "Rascall—disregardful of any Engagement of Words or Oaths not bound by penalties." Washington demanded a second meeting, and Clifton refused to back down. But apparently he had no more loyalty to Mason than he did to Washington. The master of Mount Vernon topped Mason's bid by £10 and finally completed the contract. He later bought 238 adjacent acres from George Brent to create River Farm, the largest (and some say most beautiful) of the five adjoining farms that made up the Mount Vernon estate.

In a short five years, Washington had doubled the size of a property he did not technically own, using mostly borrowed funds from the nation he would later defeat in the Revolutionary War. It was not difficult to convince London agents to establish lines of credit based on future sales of tobacco.

In 1761, Washington's brother's widow, Ann Fairfax Washington, died and the full Mount Vernon estate transferred to Washington's ownership. He soon negotiated deals with four other neighbors, quickly expanding his property by another 548 acres. His tobacco crops had not been as profitable as expected, however, and his London agents became impatient with Washington's deepening debts.

Washington was one of the first farmers to wean himself away from the tobacco business (an enterprise that was controlled by notorious London merchants), in favor of wheat and other crops. As a result, his bank accounts gradually began to flourish, and his fervor for real estate returned after a brief lull.

Unlike real estate investors of today, Washington probably believed that there were more important factors than "location, location, location." The timing of purchases was equally important. More than once, for instance, Washington offered to purchase adjacent land when he knew a neighbor was facing a financial crisis.

Does this sound a little heartless? There's no denying that Washington was seldom sentimental when it came to business ventures. But he never crossed the line and pushed too far—in fact, we know of times when he tried to *help* a neighbor in distress, rather than exploit his ill fortune.

Captain John Posey was not just a neighbor, but also one of Washington's good friends. The two men chased foxes together and probably celebrated the capture of their prey (or not) with some gusto. Posey was known for spending too much time on drinking and carousing and too little time on managing his affairs. He asked for—and was given—several loans from his friend Washington (as well as many others), but his debts continued to grow.

When Posey's other creditors demanded to be paid, the court ordered most of his estate to be sold at auction. At the auction, Washington acquired 200 prime acres, but he still craved the 6 acres that surrounded Posey's home, which Posey had been allowed to keep. From this small slice of land on the Potomac, Posey had somehow managed to sustain a successful ferry and an established fishery.

But the old dog kept to his old tricks, and Posey again became saddled with debt. Once more, he asked Washington for a loan. This time, however, Washington purchased Posey's homestead, ferry, and fishery for the bargain-basement price of £50. Posey packed his bags and moved away. Interestingly, he almost seemed to drop off the face of the earth—Washington apparently never heard from him, or of him, again.

Washington continued to expand his estate by adding bits and pieces, securing the last major tract from Penelope French in 1786. Ultimately, his plantation spanned 12 square miles and included four working farms. More than 300 people called Mount Vernon home.

Washington's land at Mount Vernon, though, was just one part of a considerable real estate empire that consumed a great deal of Washington's time and interest. Even later in life, Washington would maintain a reputation as a hard-nosed negotiator who seldom allowed sentimentality to cloud his judgment. For instance, when he learned that squatters had taken up residence on some of his land in the western territories—land he had not laid eyes on for years and used for no purpose whatsoever—he insisted that offi-cials take action to remove the intruders posthaste. And they did. Simply put, the law was on his side, and he made good use of it.

Washington's writings reveal that he had hopes of devel-oping more of his land holdings for agricultural purposes. But his service in the Revolutionary War and as president took so much of his time and energy that he never followed through on his grand plans.

However, it seems that a large percentage of his holdings beyond the gates of Mount Vernon were simply speculative investments, mostly in the areas north and west of Mount Vernon. Not only did Washington own almost 8,000 acres at Mount Vernon, but he owned more than 2,700 acres in Loudoun County, Virginia, nearly 1,000 acres in Fauquier County, more than 2,000 acres in Berkeley County (now in West Virginia), 4,000 acres of the Dismal Swamp, and small tracts in Frederick, Hampshire (also in West Virginia), Gloucester, and Suffolk Counties. In Alexandria, he owned a half-acre lot and a full-fledged townhouse. He owned a lot in Winchester, two in Warm Springs, six in the Richmond area, one near Williamsburg, and three near Fredericksburg. He owned two townhouses on Capitol Hill and at least four other lots in the federal city. Add to that more than 33,000 acres in the Ohio Valley, more than 1,000 acres in Maryland, 5,000 acres in Kentucky, and 3,000 acres near the site of present-day Cincinnati. The grand total of Washington's holdings approached 70,000 acres.[2]

Washington's passion for more and more land sometimes caused his cash reserves to shrink to precarious levels. In the spring of 1789, after he was informed of his election as the first president of the United States, Washington made a celebrated journey from Mount Vernon to New York City for an elaborate inauguration. There were a variety of festive celebrations along the way, but his very first stop was a bank in Alexandria, so that he could borrow much-needed cash for the journey.

It is a challenge to compare the wealth of different generations over a period of two centuries, but when scholars and economists have made this attempt, they often determine that Washington was our most affluent president. If so, this evaluation is based almost solely on Washington's land holdings—they were indeed vast and varied.

In terms of real estate, Washington may have been ahead of his time. More than any other Founding Father, he knew instinctively that America was bound for glory. He believed deeply in republican government and the free enterprise system, and felt that only time stood in the way of America's march toward becoming a world power. But he underestimated the time it would take for land values to escalate. On the tiny island of Britain, land was at a premium and labor was plentiful. In eighteenth-century America, expansion westward made acreage plentiful, and the only viable labor force for major landowners in the south was slavery.

So as Washington became older and wiser, his love of the land and his growing revulsion for slavery came to be more and more at odds with each other. When he retired from the presidency, Washington returned to Mount Vernon with the hope of renting much of his Mount Vernon land to tenant farmers who would, in turn, hire Mount Vernon slaves he eventually hoped to free. Alas, it seems that no one answered his advertisements. Mount Vernon's soil was not especially fertile, and potential renters found better values elsewhere.

In the final years of his life, Washington probably did his fair share of soul-searching. If he followed through with his plans to free his slaves, how would the plantation he spent 40 years nurturing remain economically viable?

Washington's decision to free his slaves in his will was a

complicated one. But it would seem that Washington's determination to assume the higher moral ground took precedence over his love for his own plantation. Perhaps he was attempting, at the last minute, to safeguard his reputation among future generations. Still, eight presidents who followed Washington owned slaves, and none decided to set them free.

Once again, if belatedly, he set an example for others to follow—even if they chose not to heed his initiative.

Farming: Washington's "Granary for the World"

Farming was much more than an occupation for George Washington. He truly loved the land and never ceased to express delight and amazement at what it could produce. The former longtime senator from the farm-belt state of Kansas, Nancy Kassebaum Baker, describes quite eloquently Washington's rather intimate relationship with his farm:

> Although he spent nearly half his adult life away from his Mount Vernon farms, serving his country as commander in chief and president, Washington always preferred to be wading through his fields of wheat. Was it ready for harvest? He would snatch the head of a plant, rub the kernels between his hands, and let the chaff blow away in the breeze. Biting down on the grain—a palpable exercise perfected by years of experience—Washington would feel the give of the shell, taste the moisture of the pulp. If the time was right, he would then summon all his field hands, as well as carpenters, painters and masons, to get the grain in.[3]

It was not in Washington's nature to approach anything in a hesitant or halfhearted fashion—like most entrepreneurs, he thought big. When it came to agriculture, Washington believed that his agricultural experiments would establish much more than the size of his harvest or the balance in his bank account. Washington believed that with land as plentiful as it was in America—even though it was by no means the most fertile land on earth—farming could become the backbone of a new world-class economy. He set his sights high, proclaiming that "some day . . . we shall become a storehouse and granary for the world."[4]

Washington was more practitioner than theorist. What would best serve America's future was "a course of experiments by intelligent and observant farmers," he told his peers. And Washington knew that he had to lead the way. "The common farmer will not depart from the old road 'till the new one is made so plain and easy that he is sure it cannot be mistaken," noted Washington. He made it clear that "gentlemen with leisure time" should accept the responsibility of experimenting with new practices, to benefit themselves and, far more importantly, the nation.[5]

When it came to planting crops, making money in the eighteenth century was a challenging and difficult endeavor. The beauty of the Mount Vernon estate belies the fact that the soil was far from fertile. For nearly 45 years, Washington tried countless combinations of crops and fertilizers, approaching agriculture in a dynamic and systematic fashion. Unlike most of his contemporaries, he was determined to renew the land, rather than exhausting one field and moving to another.

Like almost all Virginia plantation owners in the 1750s, the young Washington devoted most of his fields to tobacco. But he quickly determined that tobacco rapidly depleted the soil of virtually all its nutrients. So Washington experimented with more than 100 other crops, including several varieties of grasses, alfalfa, buckwheat, winter vetch, potatoes, oats, and red and white clover.[6] He also conducted trials of all sorts of fertilizers, including tree mold, fish heads, and the rich mud from the bottom of the Potomac River.

Like the good surveyor he was, Washington took pen, paper, compass, and ruler in hand, divided up his fields, and placed adjacent tracts on different crop rotation schedules. He tried dozens of formulas, ultimately selecting a seven-year crop rotation system that he felt maximized profits without ruining the soil. The first year he planted wheat. The second year he planted buckwheat for green manure, plowing it under. The third year he again planted wheat, followed by three successive plantings of grass and clover. While the land restored itself, he used the pasture to fatten livestock. The final crop in the seven-year cycle was usually corn or potatoes.

In hindsight, Washington's formula had many flaws. It favored the land far more than his pocketbook, producing only three cash crops in seven years. But Washington was a pioneer in an age when most farmers were ruining their fields, and eventually their bank accounts. He was determined to break away from the one-crop system, and, without question, he succeeded.

Like other entrepreneurs in the nascent stages of a new business venture, Washington often invested in new equipment. He wrote to William Pearce, one of his farm managers, that he intended to furnish his farms with "every kind of Tool and implement that is calculated to do good and neat work."[7] But occasionally Washington threw up his hands in frustration and decided to turn to his own creative mind to solve an especially perplexing problem.

When he was only 28 years old, Washington wrote in his diary that he "spent the greatest part of the day in making a new plow of my own invention."[8] The exact design of this particular plow is not known, but about 25 years later, we know that Washington did indeed design and manufacture an improved version of what was referred to as a "barrel plow."

In Washington's time, the average farmer was planting seeds the way farmers had done for decades, if not centuries. The backbreaking process of distributing seeds into a furrow by hand, then pulling or pushing dirt over them with a hoe, drag, or harrow, struck Washington as archaic. Washington's new barrel seeder, loosely based on designs from two popular books of the period, started with a simple cylinder with carefully calibrated holes, mounted onto a plow with wheels. A horse pulled the plow forward, the barrel rotated, and seeds tumbled out into tubes that distributed them into the furrow.

In all likelihood, Washington had to adjust the different aspects of the barrel plow many times before it began to distribute the right amount of seed in a consistent manner, but this represented just the kind of challenge that Washington relished.

His attention to detail was legendary, which probably made him, for most people, a difficult man to work for. Still, one has to admire a busy man like Washington, who somehow found the time to figure out that a bushel of timothy seeds included on average 3,410,000 individual kernels.

Although wheat developed into Washington's most profitable crop, he was keenly disappointed that the processing of the grain was once again an ancient ritual that reflected none of the inventiveness and creativity of modern farming. At harvest time, slaves gathered the wheat stalks onto wooden floorboards or, in some cases, on the earth itself, before striking it with crude wooden flails to break the grain from the chaff. Washington also used workhorses, tethered to travel in a circular pattern, to tread on the wheat. Their huge hoofs effectively separated the grain, but it was a messy process, particularly if the weather failed to cooperate.

In 1792, Washington decided to make a major investment that he hoped would revolutionize the processing of wheat by bringing the treading activity indoors. He designed and constructed a 16-sided, two-story barn that reflected a willingness to risk significant dollars in what business executives would describe today as "research and development."

Washington's brick-and-wood barn included an earthen ramp so that horses could enter a door to the second floor. The wheat was placed on the floor around the outer edge of the barn so that the horses could continue to move in a circular path. This was important, because horses generally refrain from urinating when kept in constant motion.

The secret of Washington's success was the carefully measured spaces between the floorboards. The slots were large enough to encourage the grain to fall through to the first floor below, but narrow enough to prevent most of the chaff from following. Like the holes in his barrel seeder, the slots in the floor were probably a hit-or-miss operation that had to be adjusted and tested, time and time again. What most would describe as a tedious or frustrating chore was probably an adventure for Washington. What could be more fun? More importantly, Washington believed that the entire experiment had far-reaching implications. After all, if grain could be processed more efficiently, America could indeed become the breadbasket to the world.

Washington the farmer was a happy scientist in a constantly changing laboratory. It is no wonder that visitors to his estate often commented that they had witnessed the most advanced agricultural pursuits in America or, in some cases, the world.

Subsidiary Businesses: Always Looking to Diversify

With 8,000 contiguous acres of land, access to a major river and several vibrant streams, and the labor of some 150 working-age slaves, Washington knew that his resources could support far more than the harvesting of a few cash crops. The downside of straightforward agriculture was its seasonality, its dependence on weather, and prices that fluctuated with the market. There were incentives for plantation owners to diversify their income streams by developing business ventures that would take advantage of the rapid growth and burgeoning economy of the new nation.

Washington's approach to these ventures was remarkably consistent. In modern terms, his business philosophy would include the following edicts:

> ➤ *Think big.* Large-scale operations seldom intimidated Washington, and he understood economies of scale.
> ➤ *Use the latest technologies,* even if it costs more. Washington kept a close watch on the bottom line, but he was also future-oriented. Mount Vernon was a "research and development" laboratory for the nation.
> ➤ *Seek expert advice.* Just as Washington liked to use the most advanced and sophisticated equipment, he also sought the most experienced managers and designers.
> ➤ *Think globally.* Particularly for someone who had stepped off American soil on only one occasion, Washington sought to distribute his products to faraway places.

Again, what is so surprising about Washington's success with his fishing, milling, and distilling operations is the limited amount of time he had to devote to these ventures. From 1775 until 1783, he was engaged entirely in the Revolutionary War. In the years that followed, he was one of the driving forces behind the creation and ratification of the Constitution, which soaked up months of time and effort in the late 1780s. He served as first president from 1789 until 1797, and his retirement at Mount Vernon was brief. He died on December 14, 1799.

With the absence of modern modes of communication, long-distance management was an incredibly poor substitute for a detail-oriented chief executive like Washington. But somehow he usually prevailed.

When Washington peered across the mile-wide expanse of the Potomac River in front of his mansion, he saw much more than a breathtaking view. "The borders of the estate are washed by more than ten miles of tidewater, the whole shore, in fact, is one entire fishery," wrote Washington. "A river well stocked with various kinds of fish at all seasons of the year, and in the spring with shad, herring, bass, carp, perch, sturgeon, etc., in great abundance."[9]

An entrepreneur like Washington recognized that the Potomac provided a tremendous opportunity, but in the modern sense, this opportunity needed to be translated into a formal business plan.

Timing was essential, for instance, because the most prolific fishing season was relatively short—about six weeks each spring, when millions of shad and herring swam upstream to spawn. Once caught, Washington had a brief window to preserve the fish before they spoiled. Distribution was also a chore, because throughout his life, he mistrusted the middlemen who often served as his agents.

These were the types of challenges that Washington relished and that he attacked with great vigor. Fishing was an important business at Mount Vernon for some 30 years, and during times when bad weather or market fluctuations caused agricultural profits to plummet, Washington's fishing operation clearly helped to balance the plantation budget.

When it came to fishing, Washington's first concern was the quality of his seine, a huge net that stretched as far as 450 feet across the river to catch the migrating fish rushing north. Like many of the items that Washington was inclined to order from England, these nets often failed to meet his very detailed specifications. In a letter written to Bradshaw and Davidson, a firm in London, Washington complained, "The seine I had from you last year had two faults, one of which is that of having the meshes too open in the middle." Washington goes on to describe exactly what he wants: a seine 80 fathoms long, 12 feet deep at the center, and 7 feet deep at the sides. (As large as this seems, it pales in comparison to nets used in the early twentieth century, which stretched up to five miles in length.)[10]

Although the technique of using a seine could hardly be simpler, the scale of the operation made it a demanding one, in terms of both the physical labor required and the importance of teamwork. J.U. Niemcewicz, a Polish noble who visited Mount Vernon in 1798, saw Washington's operation first-hand, noting that "about 100,000 are caught at a time."[11]

Dennis Pogue, Mount Vernon's expert on the topic, describes the process this way:

Washington's fishing operation consisted of small boats using long seine nets to catch and haul ashore fish as they made their annual spring migration. The boat, powered by two men using oars, would row out into the river following a semi-circular path. The seine, as much as 450 feet long and with lead weights attached to one edge and corks tied to the opposite side, was let out over the stern as the vessel traveled in its arc. Hauling lines, or ropes up to 1500 feet in length, were attached to the two ends of the seine, which the boat brought back to other workers waiting on shore. The fishermen would haul in on the lines, causing the seine to close and trap the fish. After the seine reached the shallows, the workers waded into the water to retrieve the fish and deposit them into bushel baskets. Once caught and cleaned, the fish were salted and packed into barrels to be preserved. If well packed and salted, this method of preservation allowed the fish to remain edible for as long as a year.[12]

Washington was closely involved with every aspect of the operation—he was clearly a hands-on manager. For instance, he noted, "Liverpool salt is inadequate" to preserve his herring. The salt from Lisbon, though usually more expensive, was "the proper kind."[13]

With such an abundance of fish, Washington had to be creative in his distribution. He would use salted fish in his daily rations for Mount Vernon's slaves throughout the year, allocating 20 fish per month per person. But that translates to some 75,000 fish each year—a paltry percentage of the 1.5 million shad and herring his fishing operation could produce in a banner year.

Washington sold large quantities to local merchants, who would distribute the fish throughout the region. Some fish were shipped to New England ports, but an even more dependable market was the Caribbean, where salt fish were traded for delicacies like coconuts, oranges, and pineapples, as well as sugar and rum.

Washington also believed that fish were a first-rate fertilizer, and once again, he insisted that his overseers keep careful records of the application of both fresh and salted fish. Would one be more effective than the other? When it came to experiments with fertilizer, Washington generally saw the glass as half full. He observed, "[T]he corn that is manured with fish, though it does not appear to promise much at first, may nevertheless be fine."[14]

Washington's fishing operation was not as foolproof and dependable as it may have appeared, however, because Mother

Nature still held the upper hand. "It has always been observed that in cold and windy weather the fish keep in deep water and are never caught in numbers," he noted. Some years, he added, the "small hauls will hardly pay the wear and tear of the seine and the hire of the hands."[15]

In addition, Washington never found an overseer he could trust with the entire operation, and he was frustrated that his workforce was not as careful as it should have been. Merchants sometimes complained that the salting process had broken down and that the barrels "were filled up with really spoiled herring."[16]

Still, Washington's reputation in the industry was good by comparison. Although he was not known as someone who often patted himself on the back, Washington once described his fish as "equal if not superior to any that is transported from this country."[17]

Washington's most important cash crop, wheat, provided considerably more moneymaking options than the Potomac River. It was here that Washington's astute business instincts were revealed in full force, as he exerted a strong degree of control over how his wheat was grown, processed, and distributed.

If the market for unprocessed wheat was unusually brisk, Washington never hesitated to sell it straight from the field. But in more years than not, he decided that his wheat and corn were more valuable when transformed into flour, meal, or liquor, oftentimes sold directly to the consumer.

When Washington assumed full control of the Mount Vernon estate in 1754, among the buildings on the property was a simple gristmill, almost certainly in poor condition due to the extended illness of his older half-brother Lawrence, the previous owner. Washington used the mill for the next 15 years and then decided that a modernization of it was not worth the expense and effort. He opted instead to build a new, much larger and more efficient mill, one with the capacity to handle not only the grain grown in his fields, but also that of his neighbors.

The construction of a mill was one of the most complicated projects on a period plantation, in part due to the necessity of creating an almost continuous source of water—and lots of it. Washington charged his men to dig a millrace and divert water from both Piney Creek and Dogue Run to the path of the mile-long tract. The digging took months, and at one point, Washington became impatient. Apparently he then offered financial incentives to those who would "be brisk and stick to it." The pace quickened only slightly, however, and he ended up pulling slaves from other parts of the estate to supplement his workforce.[18]

Meanwhile, local rock was gathered and stone was quarried to serve as the foundation and walls for the new building.

It is no surprise that Washington wanted the highest-quality equipment for his mill, starting with the world's best millstones imported from France. Generally used at commercial mills, these stones were especially hard and dense, so they maintained a sharp cutting edge far longer.

Almost 20 years after this mill was constructed, Washington decided to implement a major upgrade, becoming one of the first businessmen in America to purchase the rights to install a patented mechanical system designed by Oliver Evans, a well-known engineer and inventor in Delaware.

Evans's approach to improving a traditional mill would be incredibly popular today because it used one source of energy—the waterwheel itself—to power a complex series of gears, drives, belts, and elevators. Virtually every aspect of the mill became automated, reducing dramatically the need for hundreds of hours of backbreaking labor.

The flow of water—a "free" source of energy—powered a

series of actions that defined the inner workings of a complicated machine. The Evans apparatus was recently re-created and installed in a replica of Washington's mill, located at its original spot on Dogue Run farm. Visitors to Mount Vernon can actually watch the Evans machinery in action and marvel at Washington's determination to reduce the need for human labor, despite the presence of more than 300 slaves.

The chief miller at the replica of Washington's mill, Joel Nichols, can manage this complicated machine almost single-handedly—which was what made the Evans system so attractive to George Washington. Nichols outlined the following steps in the process:

1. A wagon is backed up to a ground-floor door and sacks of grain are tossed to the floor.
2. A worker pours the grain into a large hopper, which drops it into a crude elevator, which, in turn, lifts the grain three floors into storage bins on the top floor.
3. The grain is then gravity-fed to a device called a rolling screen, also run by water-powered belts, which filters out dirt and larger particles of trash and chaff.
4. The cleaned grain then descends another floor by way of a narrow chute, which leads to another hopper, which leads to the shoe. The shoe regulates the speed of the flow of grain into the eye of the top stone.
5. The French stones grind the grain as finely as possible, and the resulting flour falls into a chute, then into a hopper on the floor below.
6. Another conveyor belt transports the still-warm flour three stories up, where it drops onto a large flat area of the floor below.
7. A set of rotating arms sweeps the fresh flour evenly in a circular motion toward the center, to allow it to cool and dry.

Called a "hopper boy," this machine eventually pushes the flour to the center of the circle, where it falls through a hole into a bolter below.

8. Inside the bolter, different grades of flour are sorted according to fineness, and then each batch falls into chutes that lead to barrels used for shipping.

The Evans machinery almost certainly needed constant adjustment, so an experienced miller was an essential part of a successful operation.

Washington complained that this job was hard to fill, despite what he clearly felt was an attractive salary. Washington knew that the installation of the Evans system required him to invest in a higher quality of management. He made up for this expenditure, however, by eliminating the need for much of the physical labor generally associated with the milling process.

Washington was able to sell four grades of products, including "superfine" flour, the purest and most finely ground available. A barrel of what modern cooks might call "gourmet" flour would sell for up to $9, while Washington's low-end flour mixture fetched a bargain-basement price of $1.50.

Clearly, the Evans equipment represented a huge financial investment for Washington, and because he was only the third farmer in America to test the system, the risk involved was considerable. Records seem to indicate that the investment paid off, however, as Washington increased his production considerably. The quality of his flour and meal was also enhanced, which enabled him to increase their retail prices.

Washington's mill was a big operation, reflecting his feeling that bigger is often better, especially in a nation on a fast course toward world prominence. In 1797, his mill ground some 275,000 pounds of wheat, which was shipped as far away as Portugal, England, and the West Indies. He also processed 178,000 pounds of corn. Typically, though, his cornmeal remained closer to home because it was a staple in the diet of Mount Vernon's enslaved population.

The site of Washington's mill on Dogue Run Farm also became the location of his last business venture—a major distillery.

When Washington finally returned home after completing two terms as president, he did not hesitate to express outright joy. "No man was ever more tired of public life, or more devoutly wished for retirement, than I do," he wrote to Edmund Pendleton.[19]

At first, the retired chief executive appeared eager to take advantage of "domestic ease under the shadow of my own Vine."[20] Washington noted that he had lost the energy of his younger years—he complained that he could not even keep pace with his daily correspondence. He was a little earlier to bed and a little later to rise.

But intellectually Washington remained keen, and he could not resist the challenge of creating one last business. His plan for the distillery, however, was quite unlike his approach to past ventures, because Washington did not perceive himself as the active "chief executive officer" of the new distillery. He decided he would give up his typical role as micromanager and, instead, depend upon the talent, experience, and sweat equity of one of his farm managers.

Born and raised in Scotland, James Anderson was trained to be a distiller at a young age. But when the economy in Scotland suffered a depression, he was one of many Scots to migrate to America. Although Washington's mere presence might have intimidated many of Anderson's peers, the Scot was full of confidence. Washington also appreciated that he thought in very big terms.

In 1797, Anderson converted a simple cooper's shop into

a distillery operation with two copper stills. In his first year, his enthusiasm for the business soared, as the makeshift distillery produced some 600 gallons of liquor. By modern standards, Washington's product was nothing approaching the dark and rich liquors that populate the top shelves of bars and taverns across the nation. It was not aged at all, so it was colorless and fairly rough on the tongue. But in Washington's day, taste in liquors varied little from one distillery to the next. The important thing was its profitability. By Anderson's calculations, the profit amounted to £83—a very impressive start.

In a matter of months, Anderson had written a business plan calling for the construction of a new building that would support a tremendous expansion. Two stills would be replaced by five. A large copper boiler would provide the hot water required, and dozens of mash tubs and barrels would be used in an assembly-line process.

But Washington needed still more convincing. He was concerned that this new business would attract "idlers" who "could not be refrained from visiting the Distillery."[21] He knew that his miller had a drinking problem, and adding a huge distillery to his Dogue Run Farm would only make matters worse.

Still uncertain, Washington sought advice from a rum distiller in Alexandria, whose words convinced him that Anderson's plan was worth implementing. The merchant told Washington that the current demand for liquor was "ten times" higher than the available supply. That's really all that Washington needed to hear.

The new distillery was constructed in record time, and Washington took great pride in a building that was attractive, sturdy, and, in terms of its equipment, state-of-the-art. In addition to the distilling equipment, the structure included an in-floor drainage system, an office, a locked storage room, and a pair of bedrooms on the second floor, probably used by

Anderson or his son, John, who was drafted into the "family business" when he was likely still a teenager.

Whiskey in the eighteenth century was a far cry from today's fragrant liquors that are usually aged in flavor-enhancing barrels under exacting conditions. Washington's libations were, essentially, old-fashioned grain alcohol. Taste was almost beside the point—it was the kick that counted. In Washington's time, "quality" was a term that applied to the alcohol content more than anything else. Common whiskey was distilled twice, while the top-shelf whiskey went through the process up to four times.

In the last year of Washington's life, his distillery was able to produce about 10,500 gallons of whiskey, valued at $7,674, as well as small quantities of flavored brandy and distilled cider (vinegar).[22]

Fortunately, Washington had not overestimated the new nation's thirst for alcohol. Selling his whiskey was the easiest aspect of the business, and his inventory disappeared almost as rapidly as it was created. In the eighteenth century, males 15 years or older consumed an average of more than 30 gallons of alcohol a year—more than twice that of the average American today.

Near the end of his life, the distillery helped to make Washington's Dogue Run Farm a very active business center for the greater Alexandria community. With the gristmill, cooperage, and distillery side by side, neighbors were buying, selling, and trading commodities with great enthusiasm.

Animal Husbandry: Breeding Better Livestock

As eighteenth-century visitors traveled around Washington's five farms, they would come into contact with hundreds of farm animals. Some would have been relatively familiar in the

Chesapeake region of Virginia, especially cattle, pigs, and barnyard fowl. But Washington clearly possessed a soft spot for animals, and he collected several exotic species as well, including fancy Chinese pheasants, English deer, and American bison.

Washington's approach to livestock was in line with his beliefs concerning agriculture and horticulture. He relished new experiments, seldom shied away from breaking new ground, and focused on the most minuscule details. Washington strove to increase the profits he made from selling his animals, but the bottom line was not all-important. He did not focus on a breed simply because it brought the highest bids at market. He assembled different types of animals, often from faraway places, and he sometimes criticized his overseers and slaves for not meeting the high standards of care he expected for his livestock. In addition to being an animal breeder and entrepreneur, Washington was also clearly an animal lover.

In 1758, when few Virginia plantations were homes to sheep, Washington owned 65 sheep and 48 lambs. By 1793, his flock had grown to 600. Perhaps more importantly, he had worked diligently to increase the amount of wool supplied by each animal. By breeding new and improved stock again and again, Washington doubled the wool production to more than five pounds per adult animal.[23]

In 1768, Washington conducted his own analysis to decide whether it was more profitable to slaughter and sell the various parts of sheep, or to take the animals on the hoof directly to the butcher. He recorded that a sheep weighing 103 pounds produced approximately 60 pounds of meat worth 3 pence, 5½ pounds of tallow worth 7½ pence, and a skin worth 1 shilling, 3 pence—significantly more in total than the butcher was willing to pay for the same sheep on the hoof.[24]

Washington proved as interested in pigs as he was in sheep. In the eighteenth century, hogs often ran wild through the wooded areas of plantations. Unfortunately, Washington's experiments revealed that the more footloose and fancy-free the pig, the skinnier the pig—and the less he fetched at market. So Washington devised a detailed plan to construct a closed pen with a plank floor, protective roof, fresh water, and good troughs to keep the occupants well nourished. His elaborate designs were really quite similar to the more advanced methods practiced by twenty-first-century farmers.

Washington also experimented with several new breeds of swine, especially in his later years. In 1798, records show that he was particularly interested in the attributes of Guinea swine, which he nourished with the by-products—the leftover cooked mash—from his distillery. One visitor to Mount Vernon from Poland, noted, "[I]f this distillery produces poison for men, it offers in return the most delicate and the most succulent feed for pigs. They keep 150 of the Guinea type, short feet, hollow backs and so excessively bulky that they can hardly drag their big bellies on the ground. Their venerable and corpulent appearance recalled to me our Dominican convents, [with their] so many priors."[25]

Yet Washington's greatest contribution to the field of animal husbandry was his popularization of the mule in America. Recognizing that a mule—a sterile cross between a male donkey and a female horse—was stronger and more durable than a horse, and usually less expensive to feed and maintain, Washington had long desired to promote this stubborn, but highly productive animal to American farmers. Unfortunately, the preferred breeding stock was closely guarded by the royal family of Spain, which banned the export of jackasses to the New World.

Yet Washington's rise to power and position did indeed have its prerogatives—the king of Spain decided to court favor with the most influential figure in America by sending

Washington two well-bred jackasses. One did not survive the long and arduous journey. Washington gave the remaining jackass the appropriate name of Royal Gift, and he had a number of his best mares lined up to greet the new jackass as soon as his ship arrived. But alas, once he arrived, the jack did not seem to be interested in Washington's stock. Washington was so frustrated by Royal Gift's nonperformance that he half-jokingly accused the king of "altering" the animal before sending him to America.

Happily, Washington was patient, and when the next breeding season rolled around, Royal Gift successfully mated with dozens of mares, beginning a new race of mules in America. Washington occasionally loaned his jack to other farmers, for a considerable stud fee. One can imagine Royal Gift touring the colonies with great fanfare, much like a famous rock-and-roll band might tour different cities today.

Due to Royal Gift's masterful performance, Washington was gradually able to replace most of his field horses with mules. In 1785, he recorded that Mount Vernon was home to 130 working horses and no mules. Fourteen years later, there existed 58 mules and only 25 horses.[26]

Farm animals were an important aspect of Washington's business pursuits, and he seemed to admire each animal for its unique contribution to plantation life. He respected the versatility of cattle, but also appreciated sheep, although they were far less fashionable among his farming peers. He clearly loved horses—Jefferson described him as the most accomplished rider in Virginia, and he was on horseback for countless hours during every chapter of his life. But when the Spanish jackass crossed the Atlantic, Washington did not hesitate to praise the impressive productivity of this far less graceful and attractive alternative.

Once again, Washington was always looking to the future,

and his "peaceable kingdom" at Mount Vernon had room for all types of four-footed residents.

The Canal: Washington's Folly?

Washington's most visionary project of all was designed to connect the eastern seaboard to the rough-and-tumble western territories. He dreamed of creating a viable trade route to the Ohio country and beyond, centered on the relationship between two great rivers, the Potomac and the Ohio, and their several tributaries. Once again, Washington had conceived and embraced a project that promised to achieve three goals simultaneously:

> ➤ *Personal gain* Washington had received a significant amount of acreage in the Ohio territories for his service in the French and Indian War, and its value could potentially become greatly enhanced as a result of a new transportation link to the population center of the new nation.
> ➤ *Spurring the economy* Washington hoped to create a spurt of economic growth for what he called "a rising empire" by connecting the resource-rich west with the port cities on the coast.
> ➤ *Maintaining the union* Most importantly, Washington's overriding goal as president was to enhance the unity of the states, and to prevent settlers in the West from looking to partnerships with other nations.

Washington knew that the biggest obstacle he faced was making the Potomac River navigable around five falls, the most challenging being the treacherous rapids at Great Falls. This project certainly possessed a personal appeal for Washington—it involved beautiful land and a vibrant river. It also required complicated engineering. There were many people who said it simply could not be done, but Washington seldom shied away from this type of challenge.

As early as 1772, Washington and his friend "Light-Horse Harry" Lee had attempted to create a company that would develop transportation along the entire reach of the Potomac River. These two gentlemen from Virginia had their hands tied, however. Maryland actually owned the river, and its merchants had no intention of allowing Virginians to take control of the destiny of such an important natural resource.

The Revolutionary War cut the argument short, but in his typical fashion, Washington refused to allow the idea to fade. Postwar, as he assumed his role as the most celebrated leader in the nation, Washington commissioned the legislatures of both Maryland and Virginia to charter the Patowmack Company, with Washington as its somewhat reluctant president. Unfortunately, however, the leaders from the two states—true to form—after hours of meetings, could not agree upon the specific terms.

Once again, though, Washington stepped in personally to save the day. He used his influence to attract the decision makers from both states to one last meeting at his Mount Vernon estate. In this relaxed setting, delegates were much more prone to compromise.

In fact, the gathering went so swimmingly that the participants decided to meet again in Annapolis, this time with delegates from all 13 states. This meeting, in turn, led to a still larger one in Philadelphia, where the Constitution was born. Few Americans today realize that the seeds for this great document were planted during a carefully staged meeting at Mount Vernon, and that the driving force behind the original gathering was decidedly commercial. It was the private sector that pushed first—and sometimes hardest—to develop a central government that would facilitate trade between the 13 states.

Washington invested a great deal of money in his new

company, even though it became clear early on that the project would take far longer than first expected. Washington probably knew that even if the new transportation system worked, he would not be around long enough to take advantage of the results.

The Potomac River, surrounded by wildlife and often full of fish, stretched almost a mile across in front of Washington's stately home and was generally tranquil. But upstream, just before it passed the site of the new federal city, the Potomac was quite different. Wilbur E. Garrett, an editor for *National Geographic,* describes the river that most Americans, then and now, really know very little about:

> . . . there's that other river, the rabid animal, flushed with red earth and swollen with snowmelt or frog-strangling rains. It leaps its banks, brutally sweeping all before it, leaving gouged fields and splintered forests. Such floods—which can push a million gallons a second over Great Falls—followed by frustrating drought, plagued construction and use of his river-canal. Extremes of high and low water made it dangerous or impassable all but 30 to 45 days a year.[27]

To get around this savage beast of a river, Washington enlisted a well-known inventor, James Rumsey, to design a canal system. Rumsey, who was also working to develop America's first steam-powered vessel, was a little eccentric—his nickname was, in fact, "Crazy Rumsey."

Plans called for a series of five locks to take boats around the most damaging falls, a trio of spillways into the Potomac River, a large holding basin, and wing dams at both ends of the system. A cluster of support structures grew up around the new operation, including workers' quarters, an inn, a superintendent's house, a gristmill, a spinning house, an ice-house, a sawmill, a foundry, and a general store. Christened Matildeville, this little village had the potential to become a vibrant trading center—but only if the canal proved to be a smashing success.

At other difficult navigation points on the river, such as the smaller falls at Harpers Ferry, Washington directed his crews to dig sluices, or simple bypasses, to mitigate the change in topography. At still other weak points, he called for deepening the riverbed and removing rocks that presented a danger to passing vessels.

But it all took too long and cost too much. Able workers were hard to find, and some remained on the job primarily to take advantage of a special fringe benefit—a daily ration of three-quarters of a pint of rum. Some of the investors never fulfilled their pledges to the project, and the initial enthusiasm gradually waned. The system struggled to open for business, still unfinished, in 1788. It was never deemed a major success—how much time and money the canal system actually saved for a shipper was debatable. No one who invested in the Patowmack Company made money, and many lost their investments, including Washington.

But he never lost hope in the project. Four days before he died, he voted by proxy at the stockholders meeting. One of his last recommendations to his heirs implied that the Patowmack Company could still turn itself around.

Bankruptcy was not declared until some 28 years after Washington's death. The nation's first railroad was not far behind, which would have made even an efficient canal system obsolete.

Some historians describe the project as "Washington's folly." But was it such a failure?

In strictly business terms, the answer is yes. Even though

the canal facilitated the transport of millions of dollars of goods in its 40-year life span, it never became the principal connection Washington dreamed of creating between east and west. And simply put, it cost its investors a small fortune.

But perhaps the *idea* of the canal did provide an incentive for westerners to remain loyal to the new nation. The fact that Washington himself spearheaded the project was a signal that the western territories were important—they were vital to America's future. And this elaborate system of waterways was by no means run-of-the-mill. The project's scale was gargantuan, its budget was astounding for a totally private venture, and the engineering required was cutting edge. It reflected Washington's personality and character to a tee.

Significantly, and best of all, from beginning to end Washington never sought to subsidize the project with government funds. The risks and rewards of the free enterprise system were the driving force behind the new canal system. It was the American way of approaching the project, and that's why Washington remained a true believer in its potential.

A true believer. That best describes George Washington's approach to almost every business venture.

When others might have hesitated, Washington said, "Go forward."

When others were intimidated by the strength and experience of foreign powers, Washington argued that America could lead the world. His vision was broad and grand, yet it was based upon a premise that too many modern business leaders dismiss today.

Washington never expected to strike it rich overnight or find a shortcut to success. He believed that experimentation, innovation, and, most of all, hard work, were essential ingredients for lasting success.

He believed that good leaders learn from setbacks and always bounce back with energy and determination.

But Washington's most lasting legacy to corporate leaders of today and tomorrow is simply this: He recognized that a businessperson's ethics should be no more flexible than those of a general or a president. He wrote to Alexander Hamilton in 1788, "I hope I shall always possess firmness and virtue enough to maintain what I consider the most enviable of all titles, the character of *an honest man.*"[28]

Notes

Introduction

1. "Military Leadership," *U.S. Army Handbook*.
2. David Abshire, "The Character of George Washington and the Challenges of the Modern Presidency," Center for the Study of the Presidency, http://www.thepresidency.org/pubs/dmaCharacterofGWessay.htm, 2000 (accessed August 5, 2006).
3. David McCullough, "The Glorious Cause of America" speech at Brigham Young University, http://magazine.byu.edu/?act=view&a=1746, September 27, 2005 (accessed August 5, 2006).

Leadership Lesson 1

1. Richard C. Stazesky, "George Washington, Genius in Leadership," *The Papers of George Washington, Articles,* University of Virginia, http://gwpapers.virginia.edu/articles/stazesky.html, February 22, 2000 (accessed August 5, 2006).
2. George Washington to Catherine Macaulay Graham, January 9, 1790, transcription, *The George Washington Papers at the Library of Congress, 1741–1799: Series 2, Letterbooks.*
3. *Olmstead v. United States,* 1928 (dissenting), http://laws.findlaw.com/us/277/438.html (accessed August 5, 2006).

4. W.W. Abbot, ed., The Will of George Washington, "Schedule of Property," *The Papers of George Washington, Retirement Series,* vol. 4, April–December 1799 (Charlottesville, Va.: University Press of Virginia, 1999), 512–519.
5. George Washington to Marquis de Lafayette, June 18, 1788, transcription, *The George Washington Papers at the Library of Congress, 1741–1799.*
6. Fritz Hirschfeld, *George Washington and Slavery: A Documentary Portrayal* (Columbia and London: University of Missouri Press, 1997), 73.
7. Peter Henriques, *Realistic Visionary: A Portrait of George Washington* (Charlottesville, Va.: University of Virginia Press, 2006), 154.
8. Ibid.
9. George Washington to Catherine Macaulay Graham, January 9, 1790, transcription, *The George Washington Papers at the Library of Congress, 1741–1799: Series 2, Letterbooks.*
10. Henry Jones Ford, *Washington and His Colleagues* (New Haven: Yale University Press, 1918), Project Gutenberg, http://www.gutenberg.org/files/11702/11702.txt (accessed August 5, 2006).
11. "The L'Enfant and McMillan Plans," http://www.cr.nps.gov/nr/travel/wash/lenfant.htm (accessed August 5, 2006).

Leadership Lesson 2

1. George Washington to Alexander Hamilton, August 28, 1788, transcription, *The George Washington Papers at the Library of Congress, 1741–1799.*
2. Washington's Farewell Address 1796, The Avalon Project at Yale Law School, http://www.yale.edu/lawweb/avalon/washing.htm (accessed August 5, 2006).
3. George Washington to Robert Spotswood, October 31, 1755, transcription, *The George Washington Papers at the Library of Congress, 1741–1799.*
4. George Washington to Israel Putnam, August 25, 1776, transcription, *The George Washington Papers at the Library of Congress, 1741–1799.*

5. George Washington to Robert Dinwiddie, September 17, 1757, *The George Washington Papers at the Library of Congress, 1741–1799.*
6. George DeWan, "Crafty Codes of American Spies: How George Washington's Intelligence Gatherers Enciphered Their Communiqués," *Newsday,* 2006, http://www.newsday .com/community/guide/lihistory/ny-history-hs417a,0, 6764482.story (accessed August 5, 2006).
7. Morton Pennypacker, *General Washington's Spies on Long Island and in New York* (Brooklyn, NY: Long Island Historical Society, 1939).
8. George DeWan, "Washington's Eyes and Ears: Based on Long Island, the Culper Spies Give the Americans a Valuable Edge," *Newsday,* 2006, http://www.newsday.com/ community/guide/lihistory/ny-history-hs415a,0,6502336 .story?coll=ny-lihistory-navigation (accessed August 5, 2006).

Leadership Lesson 3

1. George Washington to the Pennsylvania Legislature, September 5, 1789, transcription, *The George Washington Papers at the Library of Congress, 1741–1799, Letterbook.*
2. Edward G. Lengel, *General George Washington: A Military Life* (New York: Random House, 2005), 9.
3. Joseph J. Ellis, *His Excellency, George Washington* (New York: Vintage, 2004), 10.
4. *George Washington's Rules of Civility & Decent Behaviour In Company and Conversation* (Mount Vernon, Va.: Mount Vernon Ladies' Association, 1989), 13.
5. Lengel, *General George Washington,* 14.
6. Donald Jackson, ed., and Dorothy Twohig, assoc. ed., "Journey to the French Commandant 31 October 1753–16 January 1754," *The Diaries of George Washington,* vol. 1, *The Papers of George Washington* (Charlottesville, Va.: University Press of Virginia, 1976), 126.
7. Peter R. Henriques, *Realistic Visionary: A Portrait of George Washington* (Charlottesville, Va.: University Virginia Press, 2006), 3.

8. Ibid., 86.
9. Ibid., 87.

Leadership Lesson 4

1. *The Maryland Gazette,* March 21, 1754: 1
2. Donald Jackson, ed., and Dorothy Twohig, assoc. ed., *The Diaries of George Washington,* vol. 1, *The Papers of George Washington* (Charlottesville, Va.: University Press of Virginia, 1976), 195.
3. Ibid.
4. Winston Churchill, *The Story of the Malakand Field Force,* Project Gutenberg, http://www.gutenberg.org/dirs/etext05/mkdff10.txt (accessed August 5, 2006).
5. Douglas Southall Freeman, *Washington* (New York: Charles Scribner's Sons, 1968), 407.
6. Ibid.
7. "The Battle of Monmouth 1778," BritishBattles.com, http://www.britishbattles.com/battle-monmouth.htm (accessed August 8, 2006).

Leadership Lesson 5

1. Richard Brookhiser, *Founding Father: Rediscovering George Washington* (New York: Free Press Paperbacks, 1997), 107.
2. Peter Henriques, *Realistic Visionary: A Portrait of George Washington* (Charlottesville, Va.: University of Virginia Press, 2006), 154.
3. Alexander Leitch, *The Princeton Companion* (Princeton, NJ: Princeton University Press, 1978).
4. Ford, Paul Leicester, ed. *The Works of Thomas Jefferson.* New York: G. P. Putnam's Sons, 1904, p. 70.
5. George Washington to Thomas Jefferson, July 6, 1796, transcription, *The George Washington Papers at the Library of Congress, 1741–1799, Letterbook.*
6. George Washington to David Stuart, March 28, 1790, transcription, *The George Washington Papers at the Library of Congress, 1741–1799, Letterbook.*
George Washington to Sally Fairfax, September 12, 1758,

transcription, *The George Washington Papers at the Library of Congress, 1741–1799, Letterbook.*

8. Richard Brookhiser, "The Character of George Washington," *Imprimis*, July 2003: 1–6

9. General Orders, August 3, 1776, transcription, *The George Washington Papers at the Library of Congress, 1741–1799.*

Leadership Lesson 6

1. George Washington to Virginia Assembly, from Dorothy Twohig, Peter Henriques, and Don Higginbotham, "George Washington and the Legacy of Character," Columbia University online seminar, session 2, http://www.fathom.com/course/10701018/session2.html (accessed August 6, 2006)

2. George Washington to David Stuart, June 15, 1790, transcription, *The George Washington Papers at the Library of Congress, 1741–1799, Letterbook.*

3. George Washington to Israel Putnam, November 27, 1778, transcription, *The George Washington Papers at the Library of Congress, 1741–1799, Letterbook.*

4. General Orders, December 29, 1778, transcription, *The George Washington Papers at the Library of Congress, 1741–1799.*

5. General Orders, June 28, 1776, transcription, *The George Washington Papers at the Library of Congress, 1741–1799.*

6. George Washington to David Stuart, June 15, 1790, *Writings*, vol. 31, *The George Washington Papers at the Library of Congress, 1741–1799: Series 2, Letterbooks*, 54.

Leadership Lesson 7

1. "James Whitcomb Riley quotes," ThinkExist.com Quotations Online, <http://einstein/quotes/james_whitcomb_riley/ (accessed August 6, 2006).

2. "The Battle of Trenton," BritishBattles.com. http://ww`.britishbattles.com/battle-trenton.htm (accessed August 2006).

3. Henry Steele Commager and Robert B. Morris, *The S of 'Seventy-Six* (New York: Harper & Row, 1975).

4. Ibid.
5. David McCullough, "The Glorious Cause of America" speech at Brigham Young University, September 27, 2005, http://magazine.byu.edu/?act=view&a=1746 (accessed August 5, 2006).
6. Sergeant R———, "Battle of Princeton," *Pennsylvania Magazine of History and Biography*, 1896, vol. 20: 515–16.
7. Frances Archer Christian and Susanne Massie, eds. *Homes and Gardens in Old Virginia* (Richmond, Va.: Garrett and Massie, 1931).
8. Donald Jackson, ed., and Dorothy Twohig, assoc. ed., *The Diaries of George Washington,* vol. 5, December 1788, *The Papers of George Washington* (Charlottesville, Va.: University Press of Virginia, 1979), 432.
9. Donald Jackson, ed., and Dorothy Twohig, assoc. ed., *The Diaries of George Washington,* vol. 2, March 2–4, 1768, *The Papers of George Washington* (Charlottesville, Va.: University Press of Virginia, 1976).

Leadership Lesson 8

1. "Work Ethic," Wikipedia, www.wikipedia.com.
2. Dorothy Twohig, Peter Henriques, and Don Higginbotham, "George Washington and the Legacy of Character," Columbia University online seminar, session 4, http://www.fathom.com/course/10701018/session4.html (accessed August 6, 2006).
3. George Washington to James McHenry, May 29, 1797, transcription, *The George Washington Papers at the Library of Congress, 1741–1799, Series 2, Letterbooks.*
4. George Washington to Benjamin Harrison, October 10, 1784, transcription, *The George Washington Papers at the Library of Congress, 1741–1799, Series 2 Letterbooks.*
5. Gordon Wood, *Revolutionary Characters: What Made the Founders Different* (New York: Penguin Press, 2006), 52.
6. George Washington to Marquis de Lafayette, June 3, 1790, transcription, *The George Washington Papers at the Library of Congress, 1741–1799, Series 2, Letterbooks.*

Leadership Lesson 9

1. Thomas Jefferson, "Thomas Jefferson to Dr. Walter Jones, January 2, 1814," *Writings*, Merrill Peterson, ed. (New York: Library of America, 1984), 1318–21.
2. David McCullough, "The Glorious Cause of America" speech at Brigham Young University, September 27, 2005, http://magazine.byu.edu/?act=view&a=1746 (accessed August 5, 2006).
3. Jack Welch, *Straight from the Gut* (New York: Warner Business Books, 2001).
4. Ibid.
5. Doris Kearns Goodwin, *Team of Rivals: The Political Genius of Abraham Lincoln* (New York: Simon & Schuster, 2005).
6. "Presidential Proclamation," *Claypoole's Daily Advertiser,* August 11, 1794.

Leadership Lesson 10

1. George Washington to John Sullivan, February 4, 1781, transcription, *The George Washington Papers at the Library of Congress, 1741–1799.*
2. "New Book Recalls Year U.S. Was Born," Voice of America News, July 1, 2005, http://www.voanews.com/english/archive/2005-07/2005-07-01-voa36.cfm (accessed August 6, 2006).
3. David McCullough, "The Glorious Cause of America" speech at Brigham Young University, September 27, 2005, http://magazine.byu.edu/?act=view&a=1746 (accessed August 5, 2006).
4. Mac Griswold, *Washington's Gardens at Mount Vernon* (New York: Houghton Mifflin, 1999).
5. Jack Welch, *Straight from the Gut* (New York: Warner Business Books, 2001).
6. George Washington to Robert Morris, April 12, 1786, transcription, *The George Washington Papers at the Library of Congress, 1741–1799, Series 2, Letterbooks.*

Leadership Lesson 11

1. George Washington to Martha Washington, June 18, 1775, *The Papers of George Washington,* University of Virginia, http://gwpapers.virginia.edu/documents/revolution/martha .html (accessed August 6, 2006).
2. *Journals of the Continental Congress, 1774–1789,* Friday, June 16, 1775.
3. George Washington to Alexander Hamilton, October 3, 1788, transcription, *The George Washington Papers at the Library of Congress, 1741–1799, Series 2, Letterbooks.*
4. Washington's Farewell Address 1796, The Avalon Project at Yale Law School, http://www.yale.edu/lawweb/avalon/ washing.htm (accessed August 5, 2006).
5. George Washington to Catherine Macaulay Graham, January 9 1790, transcription, *The George Washington Papers at the Library of Congress, 1741–1799, Series 2, Letterbooks.*
6. Paul Leicester Ford, *The True George Washington* (Philadelphia, Pa.: J.B. Lippincott, 1896).
7. George Washington, "Speech to Officers at Newburgh," http://www.pbs.org/georgewashington/milestones/new- burgh_read.html (accessed August 6, 2006).
8. Donald Jackson, ed., and Dorothy Twohig, assoc. ed., "March," *The Diaries of George Washington, The Papers of George Washington* (Charlottesville, Va.: University Press of Virginia, 1976).
9. Dorothy Twohig, Peter Henriques, and Don Higginbotham, "George Washington and the Legacy of Character," Columbia University online seminar, session 2, http:// www.fathom.com/course/10701018/session2.html (accessed August 6, 2006).
10. Ibid.

Leadership Lesson 12

1. George Washington to Nicholas Pike, June 20, 1788, tran- scription, *The George Washington Papers at the Library of Congress, 1741–1799, Series 2, Letterbooks.*

2. George Washington to D.C. Commissioners, March 3, 1793, *George Washington Papers at the Library of Congress, 1741–1799: Series 4, General Correspondence, 1697–1799.*
3. Joel Achenbach, *The Grand Idea: George Washington's Potomac and the Race to the West* (New York: Simon & Schuster, 2004), 6.
4. Joseph J. Ellis, *His Excellency, George Washington* (New York: Vintage, 2004), 87.

Leadership Lesson 13

1. George Washington to Thomas Lansdale, January 25, 1783, *The George Washington Papers at the Library of Congress, 1741–1799: Series 3b, Varick Transcripts.*
2. George Washington to George Mason, April 5, 1769, *The George Washington Papers at the Library of Congress, 1741–1799: Series 5, Financial Papers, Account Book 2.*
3. Daniel Webster, "The Character of Washington: A Speech by Daniel Webster at a Public Dinner on the 22nd of February, 1832, in Honor of the One Hundredth Birthday of George Washington,"; italics added, http://mulibraries .missouri.edu/specialcollections/webster.htm (accessed August 7, 2006).
4. Joseph Addison, *Cato,* act 3, scene 5.
5. Isaac Weld, Jr., *Travels Through the States of North America and the Provinces of Upper and Lower Canada During the Years 1795 1796 and 1797* (London: J Stockdale Piccadilly, 1800).
6. George Washington to James Mease, May 12, 1777, *The George Washington Papers at the Library of Congress, 1741–1799: Series 3b, Varick Transcripts.*

Leadership Lesson 14

1. Ron Rorrer, "A Foot in the Door," *Mechanical Engineerin* May 10, 2005, http://www.memagazine.org/contents/curre webonly/wex51005.html (accessed August 7, 2006).
2. George Washington to Martha Washington, June 18, *The Papers of George Washington, Documents,* Unive

Virginia, http://gwpapers.virginia.edu/documents/revolution/martha.html (accessed August 7, 2006).

3. George Washington to Mary Ball Washington, August 14, 1755, transcription, *The George Washington Papers at the Library of Congress, 1741–1799, Series 2, Letterbooks.*

4. George Washington to William Ramsay, January 29, 1769, *The George Washington Papers at the Library of Congress, 1741–1799: Series 5, Financial Papers, Account Book 2.*

5. George Washington to Marquis de Lafayette, June 18, 1788, transcription, *The George Washington Papers at the Library of Congress, 1741–1799, Series 2, Letterbooks.*

Leadership Lesson 15

1. Peter Henriques, *Realistic Visionary: A Portrait of George Washington* (Charlottesville, Va.: University of Virginia Press, 2006), 174.

2. George Washington to the Reformed German Congregation of New York, November 27, 1783, transcription, *The George Washington Papers at the Library of Congress, 1741–1799: Series 3b, Varick Transcripts.*

3. George Washington to the Mayor, Recorder, Alderman, and Common Council of Philadelphia, April 20, 1789, *Writings,* vol. 30: 289.

4. George Washington to William Heath, May 9, 1789, transcription, *The George Washington Papers at the Library of Congress, 1741–1799, Series 2, Letterbooks.*

5. George Washington to Benjamin Harrison, December 18, 1778, *The George Washington Papers at the Library of Congress, 1741–1799: Series 3h, Varick Transcripts.*

6. George Washington to the Synod of the Reformed Dutch Church in North America, October 9, 1789, *Writings,* vol. 30: 432.

7. George Washington to the Legislature of the State of Connecticut, October 17, 1789, *Writings,* vol. 30: 453.
George Washington to the Hebrew Congregation of Newport, August 17, 1790, transcription, *The George Washington Papers at the Library of Congress, 1741–1799, Series 2, Letterbooks.*

9. George Washington to Newport clergy, August 17, 1790, transcription, *The George Washington Papers at the Library of Congress, 1741–1799, Series 2, Letterbooks.*
10. General Orders, July 2, 1776, transcription, *The George Washington Papers at the Library of Congress, 1741–1799: Series 3g, Varick Transcripts.*
11. First Inaugural Address of George Washington, April 30, 1789, The Avalon Project at Yale Law School, http://www.yale.edu/lawweb/avalon/washing.htm (accessed August 7, 2006).

The Rules of Civility

1. *George Washington's Rules of Civility & Decent Behaviour In Company and Conversation* (Mount Vernon, Va.: Mount Vernon Ladies' Association, 1989), 13.

George Washington, Entrepreneur

1. John H. Rhodehamel, "The Growth of Mount Vernon" *Annual Report of the Mount Vernon Ladies' Association, 1982* (Mount Vernon, Va.: Mount Vernon Ladies' Association, 1982).
2. *The Last Will and Testament of George Washington* (Mount Vernon, Va.: Mount Vernon Ladies' Association, 1972).
3. Alan and Donna Jean Fusonie, *George Washington: Pioneer Farmer.* (Mount Vernon, Va.: Mount Vernon Ladies' Association, 1998).
4. George Washington to Marquis de Lafayette, June 18, 1788, *The Papers of George Washington* (Charlottesville, Va.: University Press of Virginia, 1976).
5. Richard Bridgman, "Jefferson's Farmer Before Jefferson," *American Quarterly,* Winter 1962.
6. Fusonie, *George Washington: Pioneer Farmer.*
7. Ibid.
8. James Wharton, "Washington's Fisheries at Mount Vernon." *Commonwealth,* August 1952.
9. Ibid.
10. Ibid.

11. J. U. Niemcewicz, *Under Their Vine and Fig Tree,* Elizabeth, NJ: Grassman, 1965.
12. Dennis J. Pogue and Esther C. White, *George Washington's Gristmill at Mount Vernon* (Mount Vernon, Va.: Mount Vernon Ladies' Association, 2005).
13. Wharton, "Washington's Fisheries."
14. Ibid.
15. Ibid.
16. Ibid.
17. Ibid.
18. Pogue and White, *George Washington's Gristmill at Mount Vernon.*
19. George Washington to Edmund Pendleton, January 22, 1795, transcription, *The George Washington Papers at the Library of Congress, 1741–1799, Series 2 Letterbooks.*
20. George Washington to Noailles De Lafayette, April 4, 1784, transcription, *The George Washington Papers at the Library of Congress, 1741–1799.*
21. Pogue and White, *George Washington's Gristmill at Mount Vernon.*
22. Pogue.
23. Fusonie, *George Washington: Pioneer Farmer.*
24. Ibid.
25. Ibid.
26. Ibid.
27. Wilber E. Garrett, *National Geographic,* June 1987. "George Washington's Patowmack Canal: Waterway That Led to the Constitution."
28. George Washington to Alexander Hamilton, August 28, 1788, transcription, *The George Washington Papers at the Library of Congress, 1741–1799.*

Selected Bibliography

Achenbach, Joel. *The Grand Idea: George Washington's Potomac and the Race to the West.* New York: Simon & Schuster, 2004.

Bennett, William J., ed. *The Spirit of America.* New York: Touchstone, 1997.

Brookhiser, Richard. *Founding Father: Rediscovering George Washington.* New York: Free Press, 1996.

Bumgarner, John R., M.D. *The Health of the Presidents: The 41 United States Presidents Through 1993 from a Physician's Point of View.* Jefferson, N.C.: MacFarland & Company, 1994.

Callahan, Charles H. *Washington: The Man and the Mason.* Alexandria, Va.: Memorial Temple Committee of the George Washington Masonic National Memorial Association, 1913.

Caroli, Betty Boyd. *First Ladies: From Martha Washington to Laura Bush.* New York: Oxford University Press, 2003.

Chambers, John Whiteclay, II, ed. *The Oxford Companion to American Military History.* New York: Oxford University Press, 1999.

Cobb, Hubbard. *American Battlefields: A Complete Guide to the Historic Conflicts in Words, Maps, and Photos.* New York: Macmillan, 1995.

Cousins, Norman. *In God We Trust: The Religious Beliefs Ideas of the American Founding Fathers.* New York: H. & Brothers, 1958.

Cunliffe, Marcus. *George Washington: Man and Monument.* Boston, Mass.: Little, Brown and Company, 1958.

DeGregorio, William A. *The Complete Book of U.S. Presidents,* 4th ed. New York: Barricade Books, 1993.

Ellis, Joseph J. *His Excellency, George Washington.* New York: Vintage Books, 2004.

Fleming, Thomas. *Liberty! The American Revolution.* New York: Viking, 1997.

Flexner, James Thomas. *Washington: The Indispensable Man.* New York: Little, Brown and Company, 1974.

Ford, Henry Jones. *Washington and His Colleagues.* New Haven, Conn.: Yale University Press, 1918.

Ford, Paul Leicester. *The True George Washington.* Philadelphia, Pa.: J.B. Lippincott, 1896.

Freeman, Douglas Southall. *Washington.* New York: Charles Scribner's Sons, 1968.

Frost-Knappman, Elizabeth, ed. *The World Almanac of Presidential Quotations.* New York: Pharos Books, 1993.

Fusonie, Alan and Donna Jean. *George Washington: Pioneer Farmer.* Mount Vernon, VA: Mount Vernon Ladies' Association, 1998.

Gilbert, Martin. *The Routledge Atlas of American History.* New York: Routledge, 1995.

Gilbert, Robert E. *The Mortal Presidency: Illness and Anguish in the White House.* New York: Basic Books, 1992.

Graff, Henry F. *The Presidents: A Reference History.* New York: Macmillan, 1997.

Griswold, Mac. *Washington's Gardens at Mount Vernon.* New York: Houghton Mifflin, 1999.

Hall, Verna M., compiler. *George Washington: The Character and Influence of One Man.* San Francisco, Calif.: Foundation for American Christian Education, 1999.

Henriques, Peter R. *Realistic Visionary: A Portrait of George Washington.* Charlottesville, Va.: University of Virginia Press, 2006.

ng, Washington. *The Life of George Washington* (5 vols.). 855–1859. O.P.

Joseph Nathan. *Facts About the Presidents,* 6th ed. New k: H.W. Wilson, 1993.

Ketchum, Richard M. *The World of George Washington.* New York: American Heritage Publishing, 1974.

Kunhardt, Philip B., Jr., Philip B. Kunhardt III, and Peter W. Kunhardt. *The American President.* New York: Riverhead Books, 1999.

Lee, Min, ed. *Larousse Dictionary of North American History.* New York: Larousse, 1994.

Lengel, Edward G. *General George Washington: A Military Life.* New York: Random House, 2005.

Magill, Frank N., ed. *The American Presidents: The Office and the Men.* Pasadena, Calif.: Salem Press, 1986.

McCullough, David. *1776.* New York: Simon & Schuster, 2005.

McPherson, James M. *"To the Best of My Ability": The American Presidents.* New York: Dorling Kindersley, 2000.

Mount Vernon Ladies' Association. *An Illustrated Handbook of Mount Vernon, the Home of Washington.* Mount Vernon, Va.: Mount Vernon Ladies' Association, 1905

Novak, Michael, and Jana Novak. *Washington's God: Religion, Liberty and the Father of Our Country.* New York: Basic Books, 2006.

Palmer, Dave R. *George Washington and Benedict Arnold: A Tale of Two Patriots.* Washington, DC: Regnery Publishing, 2006.

Pogue, Dennis J. and Esther C. White. *George Washington's Gristmill at Mount Vernon.* Mount Vernon, VA: Mount Vernon Ladies' Association, 2005.

Ridings, William J., Jr., and Stuart B. McIver. *Rating the Presidents: A Ranking of U.S. Leaders from the Great and Honorable to the Dishonest and Incompetent.* New York: Citadel Press, 2000.

Schroeder, John Frederick. *Maxims of George Washington: Political, Military, Social, Moral, and Religious.* Mount Vernon, Va.: Mount Vernon Ladies' Association, 1989.

Smith, Richard Norton. *Patriarch: George Washington and the New American Nation.* New York: Houghton Mifflin, 1993.

Truman, Margaret. *First Ladies.* New York: Fawcett Columbine, 1995.

Unger, Harlow Giles. *The Unexpected George Washington: H Private Life.* Hoboken, NJ: John Wiley & Sons, 2006.

Warren, Jack D. *The Presidency of George Washington.* Charlottesville, VA: University of Virginia Press, 2002.

Washington, George, and Marvin Kitman. *George Washington's Expense Account.* New York: Harper & Row, 1988.

Washington, George, and Ann M. Rauscher, annotator. *George Washington's Rules of Civility & Decent Behavior in Company and Conversation.* Mount Vernon, Va.: Mount Vernon Ladies' Association, 1989.

Whitney, David C., and Robin Vaughn Whitney. *The American Presidents.* Garden City, N.Y.: GuildAmerica Books, 1997.

Wood, Gordon S. *Revolutionary Characters: What Made the Founders Different.* New York: Penguin Press, 2006.

Resources

Video

Biography: George Washington: American Revolutionary. A&E Television Networks, 2000.

Biography: George Washington: Founding Father. Hearst/ABC/ NBC Arts & Entertainment Networks, 1994.

The Life of George Washington. Finley-Holiday Film Corp. in association with the Mount Vernon Ladies' Association, 2005.

Washington the Warrior. Robert M. Wise. Cosgrove/Meurer Productions, 2006.

Web Sites

George Washington's Mount Vernon Estate and Gardens. The Mount Vernon Ladies' Association. http://www.mount vernon.org.

A Century of Lawmaking for a New Nation: U.S. Congressional Documents and Debates, 1774–1875. http://memory.loc.gov/ ammem/amlaw/lawhome.html.

The Diaries of George Washington. http://memory.loc.gov/ ammem/gwhtml/gwseries1.html#D.

George Washington. Wikipedia. http://en.wikipedia.org/wiki George_Washington.

George Washington Papers at the Library of Congre 1741–1799. http://memory.loc.gov/ammem/gwhtml/gwh .html.

The Papers of George Washington. http://www.gwpapers
.virginia.edu/.
The Writings of George Washington from the Original
Manuscript Sources, 1745–1799. University of Virginia,
http://etext.virginia.edu/washington/fitzpatrick/.

Manuscript Collections

Mount Vernon Department of Collections, Mount Vernon, Va.

About the Authors

James C. Rees has been the executive director of Historic Mount Vernon, the nation's most popular historic home with more than a million annual visitors, since 1994. He has served in several other positions at Mount Vernon since his arrival there in 1983. He previously worked on the nationwide properties program of the National Trust for Historic Preservation, as public relations director for The College of William and Mary and the Virginia Shakespeare Festival, and as a cub reporter for the *Daily Press* newspaper in Tidewater, Virginia. He holds an undergraduate degree from The College of William and Mary and a master's degree from George Washington University. He has served as the president of the Virginia Association of Museums and president of the Friends of the Potomac River. He is the author of numerous books and publications and has appeared on a variety of television programs, including the *Today* show and *CBS Sunday Morning*.

STEPHEN J. SPIGNESI is a *New York Times* best-selling author who writes about historical biography, popular culture, television, film, American and world history, and contemporary fiction. Spignesi's three dozen books have been translated into several languages, and he has also written for many magazines and contributed chapters and essays to a wide range of books. He has appeared on CNN, MSNBC, Fox News Channel, and other TV and radio outlets, including the 1998 E! documentary *The*

Kennedys: Power, Seduction, and Hollywood,
and the episode on Stephen King that aired on
A&E's *Biography* in January 2000. Stephen's
1997 book *JFK Jr.* was a *New York Times* best
seller. His authorized *Complete Stephen King
Encyclopedia* was a 1991 Bram Stoker Award
nominee.

In addition to writing, Stephen also lec-
tures on a variety of popular culture and his-
torical subjects and teaches writing in the
Connecticut area. He is a graduate of the
University of New Haven, and lives in New
Haven, Connecticut, with his wife, Pam.

Index

Abolitionists, 73
Abshire, David, xx
Adams, John, xxi, 8, 93
  inauguration of, 82–83
Addison, Joseph, 95–96
Admonitions, 127–128
Advice, 127, 136
  for Washington's enterprises, 162
African Americans, in Continental
  Army, 7. See also Slavery
Agriculture, 173. See also Farmer(s)
Alcohol content, of Washington's
  whiskey, 172
Alexander, William, 41
Alexandria, Virginia, 155, 171
Alexandria Academy, 44
Allegheny County, Pennsylvania,
  64–65
Allegheny Mountains, 23
Allegheny River, 29
Ambiguity, Washington on, 5
Ambition, in leadership, 19–25
America. See also United States
  happiness in, 101–102
  importation of mules into, 174–175
  odds against winning Revolutionary
    War, 100–101
  pomp and circumstance in, 92
  Providence/God and, 104, 105, 106,
    107–109
  public perception of Washington in,
    xi–xv
  slavery outlawed in, 7

  trade routes in, 176, 177–178,
    179–180
  transfer of power in, 50–51, 82–83
  Washington's contributions to, xi,
    xii–xiii
  as the world's granary, 157, 158
American genius, Washington on,
  87–88
Anderson, James, 170–171, 171–172
Anderson, John, 172
André, John, 13
Anger
  justifiable, 37–38
  public display of, 128
  at table, 143
  Washington's management of, 34–35
Animal husbandry, 150, 172–176. See
  also Farmer(s)
Annapolis, Potomac River canal project
  and, 177
Architecture
  of Mount Vernon, 9
  of Washington, D.C., 8–9, 88
Army. See also Continental Army
  respect for religion required of, 109
  to suppress Whiskey Rebellion,
    65–66
Arnold, Benedict, 13, 109
Arrogance, 124
  of young Washington, 83–84
Attention, 136, 140
Authority, Washington and, 15–16,
  65–66

Automation, in milling business,
167–169

Baker, Nancy Kassebaum, 157
Baldridge, Letitia, 21–22
Banking, 115
Bank of America, 115, 116
Bankruptcy, of Potomac River canal
project, 179–180
Barbados, 89
Barbarity, 119
Barn, for wheat harvesting, 161
Barrel plow, Washington's development
of, 159–160
Barrel seeder, 86, 160
Bassett, Burwell, 50
Becton, Julius, 63
Behavior, of Washington, 33–34
Betrayal
by Benedict Arnold, 13
by Indians 28–29
during Revolutionary War, 42
during Washington's administration,
35–36
Bigotry, Washington versus, 106
Blame, Washington and, 40
Blue Ridge Mountains, 22
Bonaparte, Napoleon, 82
Bosses, 139–140
Boston, 61
Bostwick, Elisha, 49
Braddock, Edward, 151
Bradshaw and Davidson, 164
Braggarts, 77
Branch banking system, 115
Brandeis, Louis, 4
Brandywine, Battle of, 12
Bravery, 152
of Washington, 29–30
Brent, George, 153
Brewster, Caleb, 18
British land claims, 23
British Navy, Washington's attempt
to join, 148. *See also* Great
Britain
Brookhiser, Richard, 34, 113–114
Burke, Edmund, xvii
Burke, James, 126–127
Burns, Robert, 33
Bush, George W., xii, xiv, 135

Businessman, Washington as, 5–6,
44–45, 57, 85–86, 88, 94, 147–181

Cabinet
Henry Knox in, 61–62
during Washington's presidency,
35–36, 62–64
Caesar, Julius, 81
Campaigning for office, 78
Carnegie, Andrew, 131–132
Castro, Fidel, 81
Cato (Addison), 95–96
Caution, of Washington, 30–31
Celebrity, 78
Ceremony, 125
Chadds Ford, 12
Character, leadership and, xx, 42
Chestertown, Maryland, 44
Christianity, Washington and, 104, 108,
109
Chrysler, government loan guarantee
for, 123–124
Churchill, Winston, 27, 30, 39, 69
Ciphers, 17
Civility, of Washington, 20, 93. *See also*
Rules of civility entries; Social
graces
Class, Washington and, 91. *See also*
Social graces
Clifton, William, Washington's dispute
with, 152–153
Clinton, Bill, xii, xiv, 135
Clinton, George, 13
Clothing
appropriate, 129–131
Washington and, 91–92, 96–98, 130
Cobb, David, 81
College of William & Mary, 44
Commerce, Washington on, 88–89. *See
also* Trade routes
Communication
in business, 15
by Washington, 14
Company, behavior in the presence of,
116–118, 119–121, 140–141
Compensation, for Washington's
military service, 152. *See also*
Salary
Compliments, 119
Compromises, Washington on, 5

Confidence, 60
humility and, 78
in leadership, xix
of Washington, 20–21, 99
Confucius, 34
Congress, 58. *See also* Continental
Congress, Second Continental
Congress
failure to pay Continental Army by,
80–82
privileges accorded to, 127–128
taxation by, 64
Conscience, 143
Consistency, of Washington, 12–13,
13–14
Constitutional Convention of 1787
Potomac River canal project and,
177–178
Washington as president of, 5, 15, 16,
149
Washington's businesses during, 162
Continental Army, 3, 85
blacks in, 7
dress and appearance of, 91–92, 97,
98
failure to pay, 80–82
Lafayette in, 60–61
Nathanael Greene and Henry Knox
in, 61–62
Washington's command of, 40–41,
41–42, 43–44, 48–50, 57–58, 60–61,
61–62. 78, 97
Continental Congress, xxi. *See also*
Congress; Second Continental
Congress
Contradiction, 140, 143
Conversation, 132, 136–137, 140–141
maintaining appropriate, 134
at table, 143
Conviction, courage of, 27
Coolidge, Calvin, 53
Cornmeal, from Washington's mills,
169–170
Cornwallis, Charles, 95
Coup d'etat, Washington in proposed,
80–82
Courage, leadership and, 27–32
Courtesy, 125, 134
Creativity, of Washington, 147
Crime, 119, 138–139

Criticism, Washington's responses to,
14, 35–36, 40
Cromwell, Oliver, 81
Culpepper, Virginia, 22
Culper Spy Ring, 16–18
Cursing/swearing, Washington on, 38
Custis, Daniel Park, 24, 56
Custis, John Park "Jacky," 56

Dancing, Washington's skill at, 20–21,
93
Daniel, Jasper "Jack," 129–130
Darnell, Sampson, 152
Dearborn, Michigan, 139
Death, 50
of Washington, xii, xvii–xviii, 179
Decision making, 59–60, 126–127
Declaration of Independence, 5, 43. *See
also* Independence
religion and, 106
Decorum
courtroom, 138–139
maintaining public, 130–131, 134
Defeat, 50
of Great Britain, 95
Deference, 78, 124, 135
Deism, of Washington, 104
Delaware River, crossing of, 31–32,
48–50
Democracy, Washington on, 5
Dentures, 96
Dependability, 99
Detachment, 138–139
Determination, in leadership, 47–52
Dignity, 121, 125
of Washington, 33–34, 35–36
Diligence, work ethic and, 53
Dining, 141
manners during, 141–143
Dinwiddie, Robert, 14, 23
Disagreement, profitable use of, 63
Discourse, 121, 141
Discretion, 138–139
Dismal Swamp, 155
Disparagement, 129
Dispassionateness, 123–124, 138–139
Dispensability, of leaders, 79
Disputes, winning, 140
Distilling, as Washington's business,
162, 170–172

Distribution, in fishing business, 163, 165, 166
Diversification, of Washington's enterprises, 161–172
Divine munificence, Washington and, 80
Dogue Run, 167, 168, 170
    Washington's distillery at, 170–172
Drinking, 142

Economics
    farming and, 158, 159
    of minimum wage, 140
Education, 70, 101
    honorary degrees and, 93–94
    Washington's contributions to, 44–45
    Washington's lack of formal, 70–71, 149
Educational assistance, by Washington, 101
Eisenhower, Dwight D., 77
Eliot, T. S., xvii
Elliot, Emory B., Jr., 35
Ellis, Joseph, xv, 21, 89
E-mails, 15
Emotion, 138–139
Employees, 139–140
    motivation of, 99
Energy, of Washington, 147
Entertaining, 142
Entrepreneur. *See* Businessman
Environmentalism, of Washington, 86
Envy, 132
Ethics, 151, 181
Europe
    George Washington and, 3–4
    Washington, D.C. and, 8–9
Evans, Oliver, 167–169
Excise tax, 64
Expectations, of leaders, 99–102
Experience, 69
Experimentation, by Washington, 86–87. *See also* Learning from mistakes; Research and development; Technology
Expertise, 124–125

Fairfax, Anne, 21
Fairfax, George, 36–37
Fairfax, George William, 22

Fairfax, Sally, 36–37
Fairfax, Thomas, Lord, 71, 148
Fairfax, William, 21, 23
Fairness, of Washington, 45–46
Faith
    leadership and, 103–109
    religious, 103–109
    secular, 103, 104
Fallibility, of leaders, 79
False teeth, 96
Fame, Washington's aspiration to, 19–20
Farewell address, 79
Farmer(s). *See also* Animal husbandry
    slaves of, 73–74
    taxation of, 64
    theft of Revolutionary War supplies from, 12, 41
    Washington as, 6, 47–48, 55–56, 85–86, 86–87, 149, 150, 153, 157–161
Farming equipment, Washington's investment in and invention of, 159–160
Farsightedness, of Washington, 147
"Father of Our Country," xi, xii
Fauquier County, Virginia, 155
Federalism, 63–64
Federal laws, establishing authority of, 65–66
Fertility, of American soils, 158
Fertilizer, fish as, 165
Fidelity, of Washington, 44
Finger pointing, 137
Firing, learning from, 73
Firmness, 181
Fischer, David Hackett, xv
Fishing, as Washington's business, 162, 163–166
Flattery, 118
Flour, from Washington's mills, 169–170
"Foot in the Door, A" (Rorrer), 99
Ford, Henry, 139–140
Ford Motor Company, 139–140
Foreign language, speaking in, 136
Foreign policy, Washington and, 94–95, 180
Fort Necessity, 40, 71
Forts, 71

Fortune, Washington's aspiration to, 19–20
France, 60. *See also* French entries
American support for, 66
Franklin, Benjamin, xxi, 33, 53, 113
Freedom, 74–75
happiness and, 101–102
religious, 106, 109
Free enterprise, 151
Washington and, 4, 56–57
Freeman, Douglas Southall, ix, 35
Free markets, slavery and, 56–57
French, Penelope, 154
French and Indian War, 23, 85, 176
Washington during, 30–31, 71, 100–101, 151–152
French land claims, 23, 28
French Revolution, 102
Freneau, Philip, 35–36
Frick, Henry, 131–132
Friendship
George Washington and, 21–22, 45–46
of Washington and Lafayette, 60–61
Frost, Robert, 77
Frugality, of Washington, 88

Gaines, Gay Hart, 22, 73
Gambling, 52
Garrett, Wilbur E., 178
General Assembly of Rhode Island, 108
General Electric (GE), 62–63, 124–125
Gentleman, Washington as, 20–21, 93
George II, King, 30
George III, King, 82, 92–93
George Washington Club, 3
George Washington's Birthday, xiii, 15–16
George Washington's Sacred Fire (Lillback), 104
Gesturing, 119
Giannini, Amadeo, 115–116
Gibbs, Caleb, 108
Gist, Christopher, 28–29
Global thinking, in Washington's enterprises, 162, 165, 169–170
God, Washington's faith in, 103–109
Goethe, Johann Wolfgang von, 91
Goodwin, Doris Kearns, 64
Government, Washington on, 4

Government subsidies, 180
Graham, Catherine Macaulay, 4, 7, 80
Great Britain
American treaty with, 66–67
inhumane treatment of prisoners by, 119
surrender of, 95
Great Falls, 176, 178
Greene, Kitty, 93
Greene, Nathanael, 61–62, 93
Griswold, Mac, 70
Growth, Washington on, 6
Guinea swine, at Washington's farms, 174

Hale, Nathan, 18
Hamilton, Alexander, xxi, 8, 79, 181
in Washington's cabinet, 35, 63
Happiness
free society and, 101–102
morality and, 108
Harpers Ferry, 179
Harrison, Benjamin, 57
Hawkins, Francis, 113
Health
dealing with persons in ill, 121, 125
of Washington, 58, 89
Hebrew Congregation of Newport, Rhode Island, 105–106
Henriques, Peter, 23, 24–25, 83–84
Henry, Patrick, xxi
Henry V (Shakespeare), 49
Hesburgh, Theodore, 3
Hessians, 49
Hickey, Thomas, 42
Higginbotham, Don, 83–84
His Excellency (Ellis), 89
History Channel, xv
Honesty, 181
leadership and, 11–18
personal responsibility and, 41
Honor, 121
Washington's aspiration to, 19–20, 41
Honorary degrees, for Washington, 93–94
Horses
at Mount Vernon, 175
mules versus, 174, 175
in wheat harvesting, 161
Horticulture, 173. *See also* Farmer(s)

Howe, William, 12
Humanity, of Washington, 41
Humility, 116, 122, 134
  in leadership, 77–84
  of Washington, 20, 77–84, 100, 122
Hunting, 52, 154

Iacocca, Lee, 123–124
Ice, Washington and, 29–30
Ill health, dealing with persons in, 121,
  125
Immorality, leadership and, xix
Inaugural ball, Washington at, 80
Inauguration, of Washington, 98, 107,
  155–156
Incentives, slavery and, 56–57
Independence, Washington on, 4. See
  also Declaration of Independence
Indians, 28–29
Inferiority feelings, of leaders, 79
Inoculation, Washington and smallpox,
  89
Integrity, personal responsibility and,
  42–43
Invisible ink, 17

Jackasses, 174–175
Jack Daniel's Whiskey, 129–130
Jack: Straight from the Gut (Welch), 72
Jay, John, 8, 66–67
Jefferson, Thomas, xvii, xxi, 8, 45, 51,
  59, 74, 83, 93, 175
  Washington versus, 35–36
  in Washington's cabinet, 63
Jersey College, 101
Jesuits, 113
Johnson, Robert Wood, Jr., 126–127
Johnson, Samuel, 113
Johnson & Johnson, 126
Joking, 129
"Journey Over the Mountains," 22
Joy, 125
Judgment, in leadership, 59–67

Kellogg, W. K., 44
Kennedy, Anthony, 15–16
Kenny, Elizabeth, 35
Kentucky, 51
  Washington's land holdings in, 155

Knowing one's place, 115–116,
  119–121, 122, 132, 140–141. See
  also Social graces
Knox, Henry, in Washington's cabinet,
  61–62, 63

Lafayette, Marquis de, 58, 60–61, 73,
  102
Lake Erie, 28
Land owner, Washington as, 5–6, 54,
  149, 150, 151–157
Lao-Tzu, 77
Laughter, 119, 129
Leadership, xviii–xx, 180–181
  ambition in, 19–25
  characteristics of, xx–xxi
  courage and, 27–32
  determination in, 47–52
  exceeding expectations in, 99–102
  faith and, 103–109
  honesty and, 11–18
  humility in, 77–84
  judgment in, 59–67
  learning from mistakes and, 69–75,
    126–127
  personal responsibility and, 39–46
  presentation and, 91–98
  research and development in, 85–89
  scarcity of, xxi
  self-control in, 33–38
  strong work ethic in, 53–58
  vision and, 3–9
  of Washington, xvii–xxi
Learning from mistakes, 69–75,
  126–127. See also Research and
  development
  by Washington, 148
Lee, Charles, 31, 37–38
Lee, "Light-Horse Harry," 177
Leisure, work ethic and, 54
L'Enfant, Pierre, 8, 9
Lengel, Edward, 20–21
Lillback, Peter, 104
Lincoln, Abraham, xiii, 64, 96
Lincoln, Benjamin, 95
Liquor. See also Spirits; Whiskey
  Washington and, 34
  from Washington's distillery, 171
Listener, Washington as, 97

Little Hunting Creek Plantation, 148, 152
Livestock, at Washington's farms, 173–175
Lombardi, Vince, xix
Long Island, 48
Losing, 51–52
Loudoun County, Virginia, 155

Madison, James, 8
Magnolia (Washington's racehorse), 51
Making a scene, 127–128
Malice, 132
Management, of Washington's distillery, 170–171
Managers, employee motivation by, 99
Manhattan, 48
Manners, 119–120, 121
  during dining, 141–143
Mao Zedong, 82
Marriage, of George and Martha Washington, 24–25, 149
Maryland
  Potomac River owned by, 177
  Washington's land holdings in, 155
Maryland Gazette, 29
Mason, George, 94, 152
Mason, Thomas, 152
Mathematics, Washington on, 87–88
Matildeville, 179
McCullough, David, xiv, xv, xxi, 49, 62, 69–70
McHenry, James, 55
McKinney, Cynthia, 127–128
Mease, James, 98
Mellon, Andrew, 44
Military, proposed overthrow of United States by, 80–82
Military intelligence, Washington's acquisition of, 16–18
Military service
  of Washington, 11–12, 23, 30–32, 40–41, 41–42, 43–44, 48–50, 57–58, 60–61, 61–62, 69–70, 71–72, 78, 100–101, 151–152, 155
Military victories, psychological effects of, 31–32
Miller, Arthur, xi

Milling, as Washington's business, 162, 166–170
Milling machines, in Washington's mills, 167–169
Minimum wage, 140
Misfortune, 119
Mistakes, leadership and, 69–75, 126–127. *See also* Learning from mistakes
Moderation, of Washington, 34
Modesty, 78, 134
  of Washington, 29–30, 102
Monarchy
  people governed under, 102
  transfer of power in, 50–51
  Washington and, 35–36, 92
Monmouth, Battle of, 31, 37–38
Monongahela, Battle of the, 151–152
Morality
  happiness and, 108
  leadership and, xix
Morris, Robert, 31
Motivation, of employees, 99
Mount Vernon, xii, xiii–xiv, 15–16, 43, 45, 73, 118, 148
  animal husbandry at, 172–176
  architecture of, 9
  entertainment of guests at, 34
  expansion of, 152–153, 154
  farming at, 157, 158, 159, 161–162
  fishing business at, 163, 164–165
  Potomac River canal project and, 177
  rebuilding and maintenance of, 88–89
  slavery at, 6–7, 55, 56–57, 74, 156–157
  subsidiary businesses at, 150
  Washington's businesses at, 162
  Washington's death at, xvii–xviii
  Washington's management of, 55–56
  Washington's ownership of, 149
  wheat milling at, 166–167, 168–169
Mules, at Washington's farms, 174–175
Murthering Town, 28

Nansemond, Virginia, 6
National bank, formation of, 63
National Gazette, 35–36

National Register of Historic Places,
8–9
Nations, religious duties of, 108
Navy, formation of, 61, 63. *See also*
British Navy
Networking, value of, 20–21
Neville, John, 64–65
Newburgh, New York, Washington at,
80–82, 96
Newenham, Edward, 108
New Jersey, 48
Newport, Rhode Island, 105–106
Newspapers, Washington and, 36
New York City, Washington's inauguration in, 155–156
Nichols, Joel, 168–169
Niemcewicz, J. U., 164
Novak, Michael and Jana, 104

Oaths, swearing by God, 107
Obstinacy, 136
Ohio River, 50
linking by canal with Potomac River,
176–181
Ohio Valley, 23, 28, 100

Washington's land holdings in, 155,
176
Opportunities, 22, 57

Papers of Washington, The, 55–56
Parenthood, Washington and, 43
Patowmack Canal Company, 45, 177,
179
Patriotism, of Washington, xi
Patronage, Washington and, 21–22
Peacetime, Washington and, 30–31
Pearce, William, 159
Pendleton, Edmund, 170
Pennsylvania, 48, 64–65, 65–66
Performance, value of, 42–43
Persecution, Washington versus, 106
Persistence, virtues of, 47. *See also*
Determination
Persona, of Washington, 33–34
Personal relationships, Washington
and, 45–46
Personal responsibility, leadership and,
39–46
Persons of quality, 131–132

Philadelphia
John Adams's inauguration in, 82–83
Potomac River canal project and,
177–178
Philanthropy, of Washington, 44–45
Pigs, at Washington's farms, 173–174
Pike, Nicholas, 87
Piney Creek, 167
Pittsburgh, 65–66
Plantations, 158–159, 162
livestock on, 173–174
Play, work ethic and, 53, 54
Pledge of Allegiance, xv
Plow, Washington's improvement of,
159–160
Pogue, Dennis, on Washington's fishing
business, 164–165
Politeness, 122
Political parties, 64
Politics
rules of civility and, 114
titles and, 92–93
Washington and, 35–36
Polls, decision making and, 60
Posey, John, 57, 153–154
Potomac River
ferry across, 57, 154
linking by canal with Ohio River, 89,
150, 176–181
mud from, 159
navigability of, 178
in Washington's fishing business,
163–164, 166
Power
peaceable transfer of, 50–51, 82–83
of religious faith, 107–108
trust and, 15–16
Washington on transfer of, 8
Washington's renunciation of, 82
Precedents, established by Washington,
8, 16
Presentation
leadership and, 91–98
of newly created United States,
94–95
Preservation, in fishing business,
165–166
Presidency
respect for office of, 135
title for, 92–93

Washington's businesses during, 162
Washington's respect for, 82–83
President, Washington as, 7–8, 149
Presidents' Day, xiii
Pride, 116
Princeton, military victory at, 31–32
Prisoners of war, humane treatment of, 119
Privacy, maintaining, 118
Profanity, Washington on, 38
Promises, 137–138
Providence, God as, 103, 104, 105
Publicity, Washington and, 36
Punishment, 66, 119, 138–139
slavery and, 56
Purity of intention, of leaders, 80
Putnam, Israel, 41

Quakers, 12, 61–62
Quality, persons of, 131–132

Railroads, 179
Ramsay, William, 101
Ramsay, William, Jr., 101
Randolph, Edmund, in Washington's cabinet, 63
Reading, 118
Reagan, Ronald, 47
Real estate, Washington in, 150, 151–157
Realistic Visionary (Henriques), 24–25
Real-world learning, 70–71
Reason, 132
Reliability, 99, 137–138
Religion, Washington on, 38, 107–109
Religious arguments, 108
Religious faith, 103
Declaration of Independence and, 106
in 18th century America, 106
of Washington, 103–109
Replica mill, at Mount Vernon, 168
Reproach, 127, 129, 136
Reputation
maintaining, 131–132
of Washington, 94
Research and development. *See also*
Experimentation; Learning from mistakes; Technology
in farming, 158, 159, 160, 161
by leaders, 85–89

Respect, 115–116, 123–124, 135
Responsibility, 133
leadership and, 39–46
Retreat, strategic, 71–72
Reverence, 143
Revolutionary War, 85, 102. *See also*
War of Independence
aftermath of, 80–82, 88–89
American chances of winning, 100–101
Culper Spy Ring during, 16–18
end of, 95
humane treatment of prisoners during, 119
importance of survival during, 71–72
Martha Washington during, 57–58
Nathanael Greene and Henry Knox in, 61–62
plots against Washington during, 42
popular support for, 39–40
Potomac River canal project and, 177
repaying debts incurred during, 64
slaves during, 73–74
smallpox during, 89
theft of supplies from farmers during, 12, 41
traitors during, 13
turning point of, 48–50
Washington in, 31–32, 57–58, 149, 155
Washington's businesses during, 162
Washington's determination to win, 47–48
Washington's mistakes during, 69–70
Washington's reputation of honesty during, 11–13, 78
Rewards, work ethic and, 56–57
Riley, James Whitcomb, 47
Risks, taken by Washington, 27–32, 39, 43–44
River ice, Washington and, 29–30
Rochambeau, Jean Baptiste, 95
Rockefeller, John D., 44
Roe, Auston, 17
Rorrer, Ron, 99
Royal Gift, 175
Rules of civility, 113–114, 115–143
Rules of Civility (Jesuit), 20, 21–22, 93

"Rules of Civility & Decent Behavior in Company and Conversation" (Washington), 113

Rules of Civility: The 110 Precepts That Guided Our First President in War and Peace (Brookhiser), 113–114

Rumsey, James "Crazy Rumsey," 178

Salary, of Washington as president, 58. *See also* Compensation

Sales, from Washington's distillery, 172

Salt, in fishing business, 165, 166

San Francisco earthquake, 115

Scale, of Washington's enterprises, 162

Schwab, Charles, 131–132

Second Continental Congress, 60. *See also* Congress; Continental Congress

Washington made commander-in-chief at, 79, 97

Secrets, keeping, 134, 137

Secular faith, 103, 104

Seine nets, in fishing business, 163–165

Self-confidence, in leadership, xix. *See also* Confidence

Self-control, in leadership, 33–38

Self-doubt, of Washington, 100, 101

Self-effacement, 78, 100

Self-importance, 116

Setbacks, entrepreneurial, 150–15

Shakespeare, William, 49

Sheep, at Washington's farms, 173

Silence, 121

Skill, leadership as, xix–xx

Slavery

in fishing business, 165

Washington on, 6–7, 55, 56–57, 73–75, 156–157

in Washington's mills, 167

in wheat harvesting, 160

Smallpox, 89

Smith, Roy L., 39

Social graces, Washington and, 20–21, 21–22, 34, 55–56, 93. *See also* Civility; Knowing one's place; Rules of civility entries

Spain, mules from, 174–175

Speech, 136–137

Spignesi, Stephen, xv

Spirit, 43

Spirits, tax on, 64. *See also* Liquor; Whiskey

Spotswood, Robert, 12–13

Squatters, 154–155

Stakes, 52

Standards, leadership and, xxi

Stazesky, Richard C., 3

Steinmetz, Charles, 124–125

Stoppard, Tom, 39

Story of the Malakand Field Force, The (Churchill), 30

Strong, Anna Smith, 17–18

Stuart, David, 36, 43

Stuart, Gilbert, 96–97

Stud fees, 175

Subordinates, selecting strong, 62

Subsidiary businesses, at Mount Vernon, 150, 161–172

Success, 69, 131–132

mistakes versus, 72, 126–127

persistence and, 47

Superiors, 139–140

Surrender, 50

of Great Britain, 95

Surveyor, Washington as, 22, 54, 148

Swearing/cursing, Washington on, 38

Sympathetic Stain (invisible ink), 17

System of Arithmetic, A (Pike), 87

Table manners, 141–143

Taciturnity, 121

Taking oaths, 107

Tallmadge, Benjamin, 18

Taxation, 64

Teamwork, 43

Technology. *See also* Research and development

in Potomac Canal project, 176–177, 178–179, 180

in Washington's enterprises, 162, 167–169, 171–172

Temper, Washington's control of, 34–35

Tenacity, virtues of, 47–48. *See also* Determination

Thanksgiving Proclamation, 108

Theater, Washington's love for, 95–96

Timing

in business, 153

in fishing business, 163

Tipping, 116

Tipping the hat, 119–120
Title, for president, 92–93
Tobacco, 153
Townsend, Robert, 17
Trade routes, 176, 177–178, 179–180.
   See also Commerce
Transfer of power, 8, 50–51, 82–83
*Travels Through the States of North
   America* (Weld), 96–97
Trenton, military victory at, 31–32, 49
Trust, 60, 99
   honesty and, 15–16
Tuberculosis, 152
Twain, Mark, 53
Twohig, Dorothy, 83–84

Unemployment benefits, 123
United Baptist Churches in Virginia,
   109
United States. *See also* America
   Chrysler loan guarantee by,
      123–124
   establishing authority of, 65–66
   presentation of, 94–95
   Washington's vision for, 4, 56–57,
      156, 180–181
U.S. Army Handbook, xviii–xix
U.S.S. *Greeneville*, 133
University of Virginia, 45
   Washington's papers at, 55–56

Virginia, 109, 148
   animal husbandry in 18th century,
      173
   marriage in 18th century, 24–25
   plantations in, 158–159
   in Potomac River canal project, 177
   Washington's land holdings in, 155
Virginia Assembly, 40, 97
Virginia Militia, Washington in, 23,
   151
Virginia Regiment, 30, 100
Vision, leadership and, 3–9
Voltaire, 103
Volunteer, Washington as, 22–23

Waddle, Scott, 133
Wal-Mart, 138
Walton, Sam, 99, 137–138
War, Washington and, 18

War of Independence, 3. *See also*
   Revolutionary War
   Providence and, 105
Washington, Ann Fairfax, 153
Washington, Augustine, 20, 148
Washington, George
   ambition of, 19–25, 147–148
   character of, xi, xii, 42
   as commander-in-chief, 79, 92–93,
      100
   contributions and legacy of, xi, xii
   correspondence of, 14
   courage of, 27–32
   creation of Culper Spy Ring by, 16–18
   death of, xii, xvii xviii, 179
   as decision maker, 59–60
   determination of, 47–52
   as entrepreneur, 5–6, 147–181
   expectations exceeded by, 99–102
   faith of, 103–109
   farewell address of, 79
   as first president, 7–8
   as foxhunter, 52, 154
   as gambler, 52
   good judgment of, 59–67
   health of, 58, 89
   honesty of, 11–18, 41, 181
   honorary degrees for, 93–94
   humility of, 77–84, 122
   inauguration of, 98, 107, 155–156
   at John Adams's inauguration, 82–83
   last words of, xviii
   leadership qualities of, xvii–xxi
   marriage to Martha Dandridge
      Custis, 24–25, 149
   as military leader, 11–12
   mistakes made by, 69–75, 148
   at Newburgh, New York, 80–82, 96
   personal responsibility of, 39–46
   politeness of, 122
   Potomac Canal project of, 176–181
   presidential salary of, 58
   pride of appearance of, 91–98
   public perception of, xi–xv
   research and development by, 85–89
   rules of civility and, 113–114,
      115–143
   Sally Fairfax and, 36–37
   self-control of, 33–38
   slaves freed by, 74

Washington, George *(Continued)*
  suppression of Whiskey Rebellion by,
    64–66
  vision of, 3–9, 56–57, 156, 180–181
  wealth of, 24–25, 45, 94, 148
  work ethic of, 53–58
  as a young man, 83–84, 148
Washington, Lawrence, 21, 71, 148, 166
  death of, 152
Washington, Martha Dandridge Custis,
    xvii, 34, 36, 37, 40–41, 56, 57–58,
    78, 93, 100
  marriage to George Washington,
    24–25, 149
  as George Washington's confidante,
    46
Washington, Mary Ball, 148
Washington and Lee University, 44
Washington College, 44
Washington, D.C., design of, 8–9, 88
"Washington's folly," 176–181
Washington's God (Novak & Novak),
    104
Water power, to run Washington's mills,
    167–168
Wealth, of George and Martha
    Washington, 24–25, 45, 94, 148
Weather, fishing business and, 166
Webster, Daniel, ix, 94–95
Weems, Parson, 11
Welch, Jack, 62–63, 72
Weld, Isaac, Jr., 96–97
Welfare, 123

West Point, 13
Wheat, 160
  Washington's barn for harvesting,
    161
  Washington's milling of, 166–170
Whiskey, 129–130. *See also* Liquor;
    Spirits
  from Washington's distillery, 172
Whiskey Rebellion, 64–66
Whispering, 137
White, Garry R., 42–43
White House, xiv–xv
Wilde, Oscar, 69
Will, of Washington, xviii, 100, 156–157
Wilson, Woodrow, 59
Winning, 51–52
Wisdom, of Washington, 34–35
Wit, 134
Women, Washington and, 34, 93
Woodhull, Abraham, 17–18
Workaholic, Washington as, 54, 148
Work ethic, 53
  leadership and, 53–58
Writing, 14–15, 118
Written rules, Washington on, 5
Wrongdoing, taking responsibility for,
    42–43

Yes-men, avoiding, 63
Yorktown, British defeat at, 95
*Youths Behavior, or Decency in
    Conversation Amongst Men*
    (Hawkins), 113